CHINESE
COOKING MADE EASY

COMPILED BY DOUGLAS MARSLAND

CONTENTS

Photographers: Ashley Barber and Ashley Mackevicius
Food Stylists: Jane Aspinwall, Rosemary De Santis and Anne Kilgour

Editor: Ingaret Ward
Designer: Ivy Hansen

Published by Bay Books
61-69 Anzac Parade
Kensington NSW 2033
AUSTRALIA

National Library of Australia
Card Number and
ISBN 1 86256 385 3
BB 90

PRINTED IN SINGAPORE BY TOPPAN PRINTING

ACKNOWLEDGEMENTS
The Home Science Department of
East Sydney Technical College
(specifically the second year
students of the Home Economics
Certificate Course) who prepared
some dishes for photography.

For fabric, tableware and background
props: Burlington Centre
Supermarket Pty Ltd, Sydney; David
Jones (Aust) Pty Ltd; Fred Pazotti
Pty Ltd, Sydney; Hampshire and
Lowndes, Double Bay; Made in
Japan Imports NSW; Made Where,
Double Bay; Magnolia's Emporium,
Sydney; Noritake (Aust) Pty Ltd;
Royal Doulton Australia Pty Ltd;
Slatecraft Pty Ltd, Sydney; The
Australian East India Company Pty
Ltd, for baskets and caneware
throughout this book; Waterford
Wedgwood Aust Ltd.

CHINESE COOKING MADE EASY

You can discover the delights of Chinese cuisine with food that's so easy to prepare and cook. Chinese cooking is famous for its variety, its subtle tastes, and its beautifully built-in balance of foods.

Chinese cooking is one of the world's great cuisines, popular in many countries around the world. Superb combinations of flavours and textures also offer the bonus of good health.

Chinese food has been described as the ideal diet for our modern times, being high in protein and complex carbohydrates and low in calories. It also caters for vegetarians and people on a low cholesterol diet. Meat plays a secondary role and vegetables, particularly the non starchy varieties, predominate. Grains are plentiful, mainly rice and wheat. Rice is grown in the south and forms the staple diet. It is also used for noodle making and flour. Wheat is grown in the north and north west, and used for flour and many varieties of noodles, which are served in place of rice.

Meats used are low in fat and high protein foods are important. For hundreds of years soy beans have been used for their rich protein, which closely resembles that of meat. During preparation, the beans are ground and mixed with water, converting them into a milky substance, then into a curd and finally a thick junket-like substance is formed, sometimes called bean curd cheese. It can be dried, deep-fried, salted, made into sauces, steamed or eaten fresh. The soy bean sprouts are also eaten as a vegetable.

Sweets are seldom eaten. The Chinese prefer savoury foods. Between-meal snacks include many delicious dumplings, steamed buns and dim sum. Fresh fruit is usually served at the end of a family meal. The few desserts that are available are usually reserved for banquets.

The format of a family meal is simple. Every dish is served on the

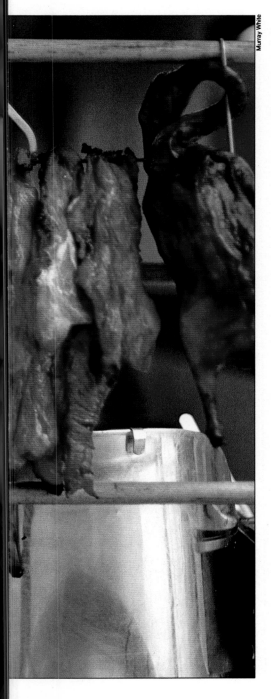

Murray White

table at the same time, not in courses as in the West.

Most modern food markets have pork, chicken and beef shredded or cut into chunks, as well as a variety of marinated meats and poultry. Chinese foodstores sell freshly roasted and barbecued pork and cooked ducks and chickens, whole and in portions. By slicing, dicing and freezing before use, they are always available for quick meals.

Many ingredients, such as water chestnuts and lychees, are available in cans, and a great variety of ready-made sauces can be found on the shelves of most supermarkets and Asian foodstores. Other shortcuts you may find useful include:

— Prepare sauces and store, unthickened in jars, in the refrigerator.
— Blend a large quantity of cornflour with water in a jar. Store in refrigerator and shake jar to mix before using.
— Prepare stocks, store in small portion quantities in freezer.
— Braise long-cooking dishes in advance. Divide into portion serves and freeze.
— Freeze fresh noodles, wonton skins and spring roll skins in recipe size amounts.
— Soak bamboo satay sticks to prevent burning while cooking.
— Always make garnishes before you begin recipe.

Asian foodstores stock many ingredients, prepared and ready for quick cooking

— Marinate foods overnight for tenderness and flavour.
— Deep-fry chow mein noodles, drain well and store in an air-tight container.
— Place cooking ingredients on a tray in order of cooking. This can be done in advance, covered and refrigerated.
— When cooking, add longest cooking ingredients to pan or wok first.
— Toast sesame seeds in a dry pan and store in a jar. Keep a stock of oven-roasted nuts to use as a garnish.
— Many oriental fruits are available canned and can be served individually with ice cream or combine several for a fruit salad. The most popular are lychees, longans, rambutan, mangosteen, mandarin quarters and jackfruit.

Chinese cooking requires more preparation time than cooking time. Many dishes can actually be cooked in less than 10 minutes.

To reduce the preparation time, many convenient ingredients are now available from Chinese foodstores and supermarkets. Rice, which is available in conventional white or brown, long- or short-grain, can now be replaced by the quick-cooking variety in both white and brown, saving 50 per cent of the cooking time.

Instant noodles are available both plain and flavoured with chicken, prawn, beef, curry or vegetables. They can be used in soups, or stir-fried with a topping. Their cooking time of 2 minutes has captured the noodle market. Dried noodles can be boiled then mixed with a small amount of oil and refrigerated in portion sizes several days before use.

YUMMY YUM CHA

Who has not sampled the pleasures of yum cha on a Sunday morning? A delightful array of delicious dishes — such as Seafood Spring Rolls, Pearl Balls, Sweet Paste Buns and Cloud Swallows — is usually served in small portions. They make the perfect brunch, whether entertaining or relaxing with the family.

LYCHEE APPETISER

565 g lychee fruit, drained
1 tablespoon salted cashews, finely
   chopped
75 g crabmeat, canned or freshly cooked
1 tablespoon mayonnaise
1 teaspoon light soy sauce
1 shallot, finely cut
2 teaspoons lemon juice, strained
red ginger or capsicum, for garnish
shredded lettuce

Retain lychee juice for sauces or fruit punch.

Combine cashews, crabmeat, mayonnaise, light soy sauce, shallot and lemon juice. Pack into lychee fruit. Top each with a thin slice of red ginger or capsicum. Arrange on finely shredded lettuce and serve chilled.

Serves 6-8

STEAMED EGG ROLLS

4 eggs
1 teaspoon cornflour
1 tablespoon chicken stock or water

FILLING

250 g lean pork or chicken, minced
1 small onion, finely chopped
3 Chinese mushrooms soaked in warm
   water 20 minutes and chopped
½ cup chopped bamboo shoots (75 g)
1 shallot, finely chopped
1 egg, beaten
2 teaspoons soy sauce
1 tablespoon cornflour
salt and pepper

DIP SAUCE

2 tablespoons light soy sauce
½ teaspoon sesame oil

Beat eggs lightly with cornflour and stock. Heat a medium-sized frying pan, grease lightly with shortening or oil. Add 2-3 tablespoons of egg mixture to form a thin omelette without holes. Cook one side only. Turn out with cooked side up. Repeat with remaining mixture.

Combine all the filling ingredients. Spread a quantity of the mixture over each omelette to cover. Roll up carefully. Place seam side down on a lightly greased plate. Steam omelette 30 minutes.

When cooked cut into 2 cm diagonal slices and serve with dip sauce.

To make sauce, combine ingredients in a small bowl. Slices can also be added to chicken broth to make an egg roll soup, or served cold with salads.

Makes 6 egg rolls

CHICKEN AND HAM ROLLS

2 whole chicken breasts
1 slice square ham steak cut 1 cm
   thick
chicken seasonings (see Glossary)
2 teaspoons hoisin sauce
½ cup plain flour (60 g)
¼ teaspoon salt
1 egg, beaten
½ cup milk or use half water and half
   milk (125 mL)
1 tablespoon cornflour
1½ cups oil, for deep-frying (375 mL)
30 g vermicelli noodles, deep fried

Remove skin and bone chicken breasts. Place each breast and the small under-fillets on a board and cover with foil. Using a rolling pin, press out each chicken piece thinly. Partly cover each breast with the fillet to make an even size. Sprinkle with chicken seasoning.

Cut ham into four 1 cm wide strips. Spread each strip with hoisin sauce. Place each piece of ham diagonally onto each chicken breast. Roll up and secure with two toothpicks. Chill 15 minutes.

Sieve flour and salt. Blend in egg and milk to form batter. Sprinkle rolls with cornflour then coat with batter. Deep-fry two at a time in hot oil until golden. Remove toothpicks and serve sliced and garnished with fried noodles.   Serves 4

Fried Pork Patties (above), Chicken and Ham Rolls (centre) and Lychee Appetiser (below)

FRIED PORK PATTIES

2 ½ cups plain flour (310 g)
¾ cup boiling water (180 mL)
¼ cup cold water, 60 ml (optional)
500 g pork, finely minced
½ teaspoon salt
pinch white pepper
2 tablespoons light soy sauce
½ teaspoon sesame oil
2 shallots, finely chopped
2–3 tablespoons oil, for frying

DIP SAUCE

2 tablespoons vegetable oil
1 tablespoon light soy sauce
2 tablespoons white vinegar
1 teaspoon sugar

Sieve flour into a bowl. Stir in boiling water with a knife adding a little cold water if necessary to take up any excess flour. When cool, knead on lightly floured board until smooth. Cover with a basin and rest 30 minutes.

Combine pork, salt, pepper, soy sauce, sesame oil and shallots. Chill 30 minutes.

Roll out dough with hands to form a sausage-shaped roll. Cut into 20 even portions. Lightly roll each portion into a ball. Roll out each ball into a 10 cm circle, with the edge thinner than the centre. The dough circles can be stacked with a piece of greaseproof paper between each. Cover with a basin to prevent drying out.

Divide pork into 20 portions. Place one in centre of each piece of dough. Bring the edges together to cover filling. Twist them slightly and pinch to seal.

Place seal side down onto board and reshape into a round patty. These may be made in advance and refrigerated.

Heat oil in a flat-bottomed pan. Reduce heat and fry patties 4 minutes on each side until brown. Serve hot with dip sauce.

To make sauce, warm oil in a saucepan, stir in soy sauce, vinegar and sugar to dissolve. Cool and serve in a small bowl.

Serves 4–6

THREE-SIDED DUMPLINGS

1 quantity hot water pastry (see recipe Fried Pork Patties)
300 g cooked and chopped spinach leaf
500 g pork, minced
¼ teaspoon salt
pinch white pepper
2 tablespoons light soy sauce
1 teaspoon sesame oil
2 shallots, finely chopped
½ cup stock (125 mL)
2 tablespoons oil

DIP SAUCE

2 tablespoons light soy sauce
1 tablespoon white vinegar
½ teaspoon fresh chilli, chopped
½ teaspoon sesame oil

Prepare pastry according to recipe. Cut dough in half. Roll out each piece with hands to form a sausage shape. Cut each roll into 18 even-sized pieces. Cover to avoid drying. Roll each portion into even-sized rounds with centre slightly thicker than edges.

Combine spinach, pork, salt, pepper, soy sauce, sesame oil and shallots. Divide mixture into 36 portions. Place one portion onto each wrapper. Join outer edges of skin over filling to form half circles. Pinch edges together.

Make a pinch pleat along each side of filling. The dumplings should resemble an apple quarter.

Heat oil in pan. When hot, reduce to medium heat. Arrange dumplings in rows. Fry until the bottom side is golden. Pour in stock. Cover and simmer until most of the liquid is absorbed, 6–8 minutes.

Transfer to platter with the brown side up. Serve hot with dip sauce.

To make sauce, combine ingredients in a small bowl.

Serves 6

BACON-WRAPPED WATER CHESTNUTS

180 g canned whole water chestnuts
2 tablespoons hoisin sauce
4–6 rashers bacon, rind removed

Drain and dry chestnuts. Mix with hoisin sauce. Cut each bacon rasher into strips long enough to wrap around each chestnut. Secure with toothpick.

Arrange on a foil-covered tray. Roast at 225°C (430°F) for 10–15 minutes until bacon is crisp.

Serves 6

PEARL BALLS

1 cup glutinous rice, soaked in cold water 1 hour (185 g)
500 g boneless pork with a little fat, minced
2 teaspoons ginger wine
2 tablespoons light soy sauce
1 egg, beaten
1 tablespoon cornflour
1 shallot, finely chopped
½ teaspoon sugar
½ teaspoon salt
¼ teaspoon white pepper

Drain rice. Combine pork with remaining ingredients. Form into 20 balls with wet hands. Roll each ball in rice until well coated. Arrange on two heatproof plates. Leave 1.5 cm space between each ball for rice expansion.

Steam covered in a double boiler over high heat for 1 hour. Serve with prepared mustard, soy sauce or chilli dip.

Serves 4

Pearl Balls (left) and Bacon-wrapped Water Chestnuts (right)

STEAMED GOW GEES

FILLING

350 g green (uncooked) prawn meat or boneless white fish cut into 5 mm dice
60 g pork fat, finely chopped
60 g bamboo shoot, finely chopped
½ teaspoon salt
¼ teaspoon white pepper
½ teaspoon sesame oil
2 teaspoons cornflour

DOUGH

1 ½ cups plain flour or Chinese gluten-free flour (185 g)
1 ½ tablespoons lard
1 ½ cups boiling water (375 mL)

DIP SAUCE I

4 tablespoons light soy sauce
2 teaspoons white vinegar
¼ teaspoon sesame oil

DIP SAUCE II

2 tablespoons tomato sauce
1 tablespoon chilli sauce

Combine filling ingredients. Divide into 36 portions.

Sieve flour into a basin. Add lard and stir in boiling water with a knife to form dough. Let stand covered until cool.

Form dough into a sausage-shaped roll and cut into 36 even-sized pieces.

Roll each piece of dough into 5 cm circles on a lightly-oiled surface. Place a portion of filling onto each round. Fold lower edges of dough over filling to form a half circle. Press edges firmly and pleat edge.

Arrange gow gees on two lightly greased plates, leaving enough space between each to prevent sticking. Steam in a double boiler for 10–15 minutes. Serve hot with a dip sauce of your choice.

To make dip sauce, simply combine ingredients in a small bowl.

Serves 4

CLOUD SWALLOWS

20 wonton skins
1 beaten egg white
oil, for deep-frying

FILLING

100 g chicken, finely chopped
100 g fish fillets, finely chopped
½ stalk celery, finely chopped
1 small shallot, finely chopped
2 teaspoons light soy sauce
¼ teaspoon salt

SWEET AND SOUR SAUCE

¾ cup water (180 mL)
½ cup sugar (125 g)
½ cup white vinegar (125 mL)
1 tablespoon tomato sauce
1 tablespoon cornflour

Combine filling ingredients. Place 1 teaspoon of mixture onto each wonton skin. Brush edges lightly with egg white. Fold to form a triangle. Place a dab of egg white on the left front corner of triangle. Join the front of the left to the back of the right side of triangle to form a swallow.

Deep-fry in oil to cover until golden. Serve with sweet and sour sauce.

To make sauce, combine all ingredients in a saucepan. Beat and stir until boiling. Serve in bowls.   Serves 4

Steamed Gow Gees (left) and Cloud Swallows (right)

Plates and fan. Made in Japan Imports NSW

PRAWN DIM SUM

500 g green (uncooked) prawns
1/4 teaspoon sesame oil
1 egg white
2 teaspoons sugar
1 tablespoon soy sauce
2 shallots, finely chopped
8 Chinese mushrooms, soaked in
    warm water 20 minutes and chopped
6 water chestnuts, finely chopped
125 g wonton skins

Finely chop prawns. Place in a bowl with combined sesame oil, egg white, sugar and soy sauce. Mix in shallots, mushrooms and water chestnuts.

Brush a wonton skin lightly with water. Using the left hand, hold thumb and index finger in a circle. Cover the circle with one wonton wrapper. Top with a teaspoonful of filling. Using teaspoon, press and push the filling and wrapper through the circle to form a drawstring effect. Close finger and thumb together to produce a drawstring effect. Repeat with remaining wonton skins.

Bring to boil 5 cm of water in a wok. Line a steamer with outer lettuce leaves. Place dim sum on top, allowing space between each one. Place steamer in wok, cover, and steam above boiling water for 20 minutes. Remove and serve with a dipping sauce of your choice (see recipes).

Note: Make sure there is some boiling water at hand in case water in wok needs to be topped up.

Serves 4

Prawn Dim Sum

NEW YEAR CAKE

The Chinese New Year is calculated according to the old lunar calendar and the actual date of the New Year changes like the date of Easter.

The traditional New Year Cake of white radish and rice comes from the southeastern part of China. Visiting is a major activity in the traditional New Year festivities in China and these cakes are taken as gifts to friends and relatives. Many families order a number of these cakes to be specially made before the festival.

1 1/2 cups raw long-grain rice (250 g)
450 g white radish, peeled and
    coarsely grated
2 teaspoons salt
1 teaspoon black pepper

Wash rice well and leave it to soak in 1 1/4 cups water (310 mL) for 12 hours. Process rice and water in a food processor to form a very fine paste (at least 10 minutes). Put white radish into a large, thick-bottomed pan and gently stir-fry without oil until the radish is soft — about 4 minutes. Add rice paste and turn the heat very low. Bring mixture to boil, stirring all the time to prevent it from sticking to bottom of pan, then remove from heat and season with salt and pepper.

Line a small bamboo steamer or a 20 cm cake tin with a wet tea towel and pour rice and radish mixture into it. Steam over fast-boiling water for 30–45 minutes. When it is cooked a skewer inserted into the centre will come out clean. Turn out onto a plate, peel off the cloth and cut into slices with a wet knife.

RICE FLOUR SHEET ROLLS

8–9 rice flour sheets, cut in half if large
200 g chicken fillet, sliced
90 g pork, sliced
1 cm piece fresh ginger root, cut into
    strips
3 teaspoons wine
2 teaspoons cornflour
1 teaspoon light soy sauce
1 teaspoon sugar
1 teaspoon oil
125 g Chinese barbecued pork (Char
    Sui)
3 Chinese mushrooms, soaked in
    water 20 minutes
1 small carrot, thinly sliced
oil, for frying
2 shallots, chopped
180 g bean sprouts

SEASONINGS

2 teaspoons sugar
1 teaspoon light soy sauce
2 teaspoons oyster sauce
pepper
1/2 cup chicken stock (125 mL)
    combined with
3 teaspoons cornflour

TO SERVE

3 tablespoons oil
1 1/2 tablespoons light soy sauce
2 tablespoons toasted sesame seeds

Combine chicken and pork and marinate with combined ginger, wine, cornflour, soy sauce, sugar and oil 15 minutes. Saute in oil until cooked and set aside.

Dice Chinese barbecued pork. Wash and steam mushrooms, remove stalks and slice. Boil carrot.

Heat oil in a wok or pan and saute shallots and bean sprouts. Add carrot, mushrooms, chicken, pork and seasonings. Combine stock and cornflour to thicken gravy and allow to cool. Lay rice flour sheets flat on a table. Place 2 teaspoons filling along one edge and roll sheet towards the centre. Arrange on a plate with sealed edge outwards.

Put plate over boiling water and steam 3–5 minutes or until rice sheets begin to soften. Remove, sprinkle with soy sauce, oil and sesame seeds and serve hot.

Makes 16

CHAR SUI

Char sui or barbecued pork, is a distinctive ingredient in Chinese cooking. It can be bought in Asian foodstores or made at home using the recipe on page 38.

DEEP-FRIED SAVOURY TRIANGLES

PASTRY

½ cup wheat starch (60 g)
¼ cup boiling water (60 mL)
1 cup glutinous rice flour (125 g)
cold water
¼ cup sugar (60 g)
60 g butter

FILLING

100 g dried prawn meat
4 tablespoons preserved turnip
1 tablespoon oil
190 g pork mince
1 small carrot, diced
3 Chinese mushrooms soaked in warm
    water for 20 minutes
3 shallots, chopped

SEASONINGS

1 teaspoon wine
1 teaspoon soy sauce
2 teaspoons oyster sauce
½ teaspoon spicy salt (see Note)
2 teaspoons sugar
pinch pepper
1 teaspoon sesame oil
2 teaspoons cornflour mixed with
3 teaspoons water

To make pastry, sift wheat starch into a bowl, pour in boiling water, stir immediately. Sift glutinous rice flour onto a clean table, add enough water to combine and mix well. Knead wheat starch dough with glutinous rice flour dough and sugar till soft.

Divide dough into three portions. Steam two portions only for 5 minutes. Allow to cool. Take out and knead the three portions together till smooth.

To make filling, wash dried prawns and turnips, soak for 30 minutes and dice. Heat a pan, add a little oil and saute pork until cooked. Add all remaining filling ingredients. Add seasonings, stirring cornflour solution to make gravy.

Roll and cut the dough into 32 equal parts. Press into thin rounds and put in 1 heaped teaspoon of filling. Fold and pinch edges together securely to form a frilly edge. Deep-fry in warm oil until golden brown.

Note: Spicy salt is made from mixing 1 teaspoon fine salt with a pinch of allspice. This dish can be frozen before cooking. To cook, defrost and cook in warm oil.

Makes 32

TURNIP PUDDING

100 g dried prawn meat, soaked in water
    30 minutes
3 Chinese mushrooms, soaked in
    warm water 20 minutes
185 g Chinese barbecued pork (Char
    Sui)
4 Chinese sausages (larp cheong)
¼ cup oil (60 mL)
1 shallot
1.5 kg Chinese white turnip, peeled
    and grated (see Note)
225 g rice flour
3 shallots, chopped to garnish

SEASONINGS

1 tablespoon light soy sauce
1 tablespoon salt
2 tablespoons sugar
1 chicken stock cube
pepper

Chop prawns, steam and dice mushrooms. Wash pork and Chinese sausages in warm water and dice.

Heat oil in a wok and saute prawns, then meats, mushrooms and shallot. Set aside.

Place turnip in a very hot wok with oil. Stir while cooking until turnip changes colour. Add pork and sausages and mix well. Sift rice flour into the mixture in wok, add seasonings and mix together.

Oil two 20 cm cake tins, pour in mixture and flatten the top with wet hands.

Place tins in a large steamer and steam over high heat for 1½ hours.

Remove turnip pudding from steamer when cooked. Turn out onto a serving plate. Sprinkle chopped shallots on top and serve.

Note: Shredded cabbage can be used in place of turnip.

Makes 2 puddings

From left: Deep-fried Savoury Triangles, Rice Flour Sheet Rolls, Turnip Pudding, a dipping sauce and New Year Cake

DEEP-FRIED TARO PASTRY

oil, for deep-frying

PASTRY

1.5 kg taro (see Note)
¼ cup wheat starch (30 g)
½ cup boiling water (125 mL)
185 g butter
1 teaspoon salt
¼ cup sugar (60 g)

FILLING

oil, for frying
3 Chinese mushrooms, soaked in
    water 20 minutes
1 small carrot, diced or 75 g diced
    bamboo shoots
350 g lean pork mince
100 g dried prawn meat, soaked in
    water 30 minutes
2 shallots, chopped
250 mL white wine
1 egg, beaten

SEASONINGS

3 teaspoons oyster sauce
1 teaspoon sugar
1 chicken stock cube
1 teaspoon light soy sauce
1 teaspoon sesame oil
½ teaspoon pepper
1 teaspoon cornflour

Peel and wash taro, cut into small pieces.

Cook in a steamer until tender, then mash well. Put wheat starch in a mixing bowl, add boiling water and stir. Add mashed taro and mix thoroughly.

On a flat surface, sprinkle a little extra wheat starch on which to knead taro mixture. Add butter, salt and sugar and continue to knead into a smooth dough. Make a long roll and divide into 24 equal parts.

To make filling, steam and dice mushrooms. Boil diced carrot. Marinate lean pork with half the seasoning for 10 minutes. Saute pork and prawns in oil and set aside.

Saute mushrooms, carrot and shallots in a hot pan and add meat, prawns, wine and remaining seasoning. Off the heat, add beaten egg to combine filling. Flatten each portion of pastry into bowl shapes and wrap filling in pastry. Draw edges to seal and deep-fry in warm oil until pastry becomes golden.

Note: Taro is a tuber and is cooked in the same way as potatoes, which may be used instead, if taro is unavailable.

Makes 24

Prawn Dumplings in Soup and Deep-fried Taro Pastry

RED BEAN PUDDING

500 g Chinese red beans
3 ¼ cups palm or raw sugar (550 g)
125 g butter
2 ¾ cups rice flour (410 g) (see Note)

Wash red beans and drain. Pour 2 litres water into deep saucepan, add red beans and bring to boil over medium heat. Cover, lower heat and simmer for about 1 hour or until beans are tender. Add palm sugar and to cook until melted. Pour in butter and stir well. Remove from heat and cool for 5 minutes.

Sift rice flour into mixing bowl, mix with 3 cups (750 mL) water. Stir batter into bean mixture gradually until well blended. Pour mixture into two 20 cm greased cake tins. Steam in steamer over high heat for 1 hour or until cooked. Serve sliced in pieces.

Note: A good quality rice flour is recommended for a better quality product. Red beans are readily available in Asian foodstores.

Makes 2 puddings

PRAWN DUMPLINGS IN SOUP

60 wonton skins
1.5 litres stock

FILLING

4 Chinese mushrooms, soaked in water
   20 minutes
3 tablespoons bamboo shoots, diced
500 g shelled green (uncooked)
   prawns, diced
200 g fillet plaice or flounder, diced
200 g lean pork mince
2 eggs, beaten

SEASONINGS

2 teaspoons soy sauce
1 ¼ teaspoons salt
1 teaspoon sugar
¼ teaspoon pepper
1 teaspoon sesame oil
2 teaspoons cornflour

Wash and chop mushrooms; boil bamboo shoots. Place all filling ingredients in a mixing bowl and mix well. Pound and stir in eggs and seasonings (see Note).

Place wonton skins flat on a table. Using a spoon, place 1 tablespoon filling in middle of pastry, bring 4 corners together and press edges to seal mixture in pastry. Bring a pan of water to boil, add dumplings and boil for 5 minutes until they float.

Heat stock to boiling and pour over drained dumplings to serve.

Note: Pounding is done by throwing the mixture into the bowl; this gives the mixture a lighter texture.

Makes approximately 60

RED BEAN PASTE

250 g Chinese red beans
180 g sugar (white or brown)
4 tablespoons peanut oil

Wash red beans and place in a deep saucepan with 1 litre water. Bring to the boil and simmer for 1 hour or until tender. Drain and cool slightly.

Puree red beans, sugar and oil in a food processor until smooth. Cool before using in dumplings or puddings. Store in refrigerator or freezer. Can be stored for more than 2 months.

Makes approximately 3½ cups (500 g)

MARBLED TEA EGGS

4 eggs
2 tablespoons dry tea leaves
1 teaspoon salt
2 cloves star anise

Place eggs in a pan and cover with cold water. Bring to the boil. Reduce heat and simmer 5 minutes. Remove, drain and run cold water over them for several minutes. Dry eggs and tap shells gently with back of spoon on all sides to crack them evenly.

Place 3 cups boiling water (750 mL) in a saucepan with the tea leaves, salt and star anise. Add eggs, cover and simmer gently for 1½ hours.

Let eggs cool in the flavoured water ½ hour. The eggs may be made in advance but do not shell them until ready to serve. Shell under cold water.

Serve halved or quartered as an appetiser.

Serves 4

STEAMED SHAO-MAI

410 g very lean ground pork
1 teaspoon salt
1 tablespoon ginger wine
½ teaspoon pepper
24 medium-large shelled prawns
1 ½ teaspoons ginger wine (extra)
2 teaspoons cornflour
24 wonton or dumpling skins

Blend ground pork well with salt, ginger wine, and pepper and let stand for 20 minutes. Marinate prawns with extra ginger wine and cornflour for 20 minutes.

Place 1 ½ tablespoons of filling in the centre of each wonton skin. Pinch edges up to make a frilly border. Leave a hole in centre to let the filling show a little bit and place a prawn on top. Place in a steamer and steam for 25 minutes. Serve at once.

Makes 24

Marbled Tea Eggs

STEAMED MINCED BEEF BALLS

3 tablespoons pork fat
1 small piece of dried tangerine peel or
   2 teaspoons diced orange rind
250 g minced beef
1 teaspoon salt
1 teaspoon sugar
1 ½ teaspoons bicarbonate of soda
2 teaspoons cornflour
½ cup water (125 mL)
1 shallot, chopped
1 teaspoon sesame paste
½ teaspoon pepper
1 ½ teaspoons light soy sauce
1 bean curd sheet
¼ cup oil (60 mL)

Boil and dice pork fat. Soak tangerine peel in warm water until soft then mash with a mallet.

Mix beef with salt, sugar and bicarbonate of soda, mix well and set aside for ½ an hour. Put beef in a mixing bowl and pound well. Dissolve cornflour in water and pour in solution gradually while pounding the beef.

Mix well with diced fat, mashed tangerine peel, shallot, sesame paste, pepper and light soy sauce. Add oil a little at a time and pound until well mixed. Divide minced beef into 10 small balls.

Wash and dry bean curd sheet, cut into small pieces and deep-fry. Put two pieces into a small dish with two meat balls on top. Place dishes in steamer. Put steamer above boiling water to steam for 8–10 minutes.

Note: Bean curd sheet can be replaced by watercress or lettuce.

Makes 10 balls

STEAMED RICE DUMPLINGS WITH ASSORTED MEATS

PASTRY

4 cups glutinous rice (750 g)
2 teaspoons salt
40 g butter
7 lotus leaves

FILLING

100 g lean pork, diced
200 g chicken, sliced
½ teaspoon chopped fresh ginger root
185 g Chinese barbecued pork (Char Sui), diced
8 Chinese mushrooms, soaked in warm water for 20 minutes
2 small carrots, chopped
2 teaspoons wine
½ cup stock (125 mL)
2 teaspoons cornflour, combined with 3 teaspoons water

SEASONINGS

1 teaspoon salt
2 teaspoons sugar
3 teaspoons oyster sauce
2 teaspoons light soy sauce
2 teaspoons wine
1 teaspoon water
pinch pepper

Wash and soak glutinous rice for 12 hours. Drain and pour over some boiling water. Stand for 15 minutes. Place a tea towel in steamer. Pour in glutinous rice and steam for 45 minutes. Remove from steamer, add salt and butter and mix well.

Combine seasoning ingredients and divide between two bowls. Marinate pork in one bowl and chicken with chopped ginger in the other for 1 hour. Remove, reserving marinade and saute pork and chicken for 5 minutes in hot oil; set aside.

Briefly steam and cut each mushroom into halves and remove stalks. Boil carrot.

Heat pan with a little oil. Pour in wine, stock and marinade of seasonings. Mix cornflour with water, add to sauce, stirring until thick. Combine well with other filling ingredients and allow to cool.

Soak lotus leaves in hot water for 10–15 minutes, wash and dry. Open flat on table, alternate a layer of glutinous rice with a layer of filling. Cover with another layer of rice on top. Fold lotus leaves to wrap into a dumpling, put into steamer to steam over high heat for 25–30 minutes. Serve hot.

Note: For a more developed flavour or to conserve time, this dish can be made up to a few days in advance. To reheat, steam till hot.

Makes 7

SEAFOOD SPRING ROLLS

20 small spring roll wrappers
1 egg, beaten
1 ½ cups oil, for deep-frying (375 mL)

FILLING

250 g boneless white fish, sliced 3 cm × 1 cm
125 g green (uncooked) prawn meat, sliced 3 cm × 1 cm
125 g seafood sticks, sliced 3 cm × 1 cm, or other seafood of your choice
125 g bean sprouts, root removed
2 shallots, chopped
1 teaspoon white wine
1 teaspoon sesame oil
1 teaspoon light soy sauce
½ teaspoon chopped ginger
1 egg white, lightly beaten

Combine filling ingredients in a bowl. Arrange spring roll wrappers in diamond shapes with the point towards you. Brush edges lightly with beaten egg. Place a small amount of filling onto the lower half of each skin. Fold lowest point of skin over filling. Fold left and right points into centre. Brush with egg. Roll up firmly and allow to stand on sealed edge.

Heat oil for deep-frying. Add three–four rolls at a time. Cook until golden; drain on absorbent kitchen paper. Serve with Sweet and Sour Sauce (see recipe) as dip.

Serves 6

100 YEAR EGGS

4 preserved eggs (available from most Chinese supermarkets)
4 thin slices fresh ginger root, finely chopped
2 tablespoons white vinegar
2 tablespoons soy sauce
¼ teaspoon sesame oil

To shell eggs, soak in cold water for 1 hour until the coating is soft enough to remove. Crack and carefully remove shell. Cut eggs lengthways into quarters. Arrange on serving platter.

Combine ginger, vinegar, soy sauce and sesame oil. Serve in a dip sauce bowl or sprinkle sauce over eggs.

Serves 4

Seafood Spring Rolls with Sweet and Sour Sauce

SWEET PASTE BUNS

OUTER DOUGH

250 g prepared yeast dough (see Note
   and recipe)
1/3 cup sugar (80 g)
20 g butter
1/2 teaspoon vinegar
2 1/4 tablespoons water
1 cup plain flour (125 g)
1 teaspoon baking powder

INNER DOUGH

2 cups flour (250 g)
30 g butter

FILLING

30 g lotus seed paste

To make outer dough, put yeast dough in
a mixing bowl, add sugar, butter, vinegar
and water to mix. Sift in flour and baking
powder, and knead into a soft dough until
dough springs back when pressed.
Prove for 45 minutes or until doubled in
size.

To make inner dough, sift flour on to a
clean table and knead with butter to make
dough. Cut into 20 equal portions.

Punch down outer dough and knead
again. Roll into a sausage shape and cut
into 20 equal portions. Place one portion
of inner dough inside one portion of outer
dough. Knead by rolling into a thin strip.
Repeat until mixed then roll into a small
round. In each round insert one teaspoon
lotus seed paste. Put a piece of paper on
the bottom of each bun. Prove in warm
place for 15 minutes or until doubled. Put
in steamer to steam over high heat for 8
minutes.

Note: Yeast dough should be made
12–15 hours before.

YEAST DOUGH

1 teaspoon dried yeast
3/4 cup warm water (180 mL)
2 cups sieved plain flour (250 g)

Dissolve dried yeast in water and leave
for 15–20 minutes in a warm place. Pour
solution into flour and knead to form a
soft dough. Cover and set aside in a
warm place for 12–15 hours.

Makes 20

SWEET RED BEAN PANCAKES

1 cup plain flour (125 g)
1 egg, beaten
150 mL water
40 g butter
170 g red bean paste
caster sugar, for sprinkling

In a bowl sift flour and make a well in the
centre. Add beaten egg and water and
mix to a smooth batter.

Heat a frying pan with sufficient butter
and make four 20 cm pancakes. When
they are cooked on both sides, lift them
out onto a flat surface to cool.

Spread a quarter of the bean paste
onto the centre of each pancake, fold in
two sides to cover the paste, then fold
over the top and bottom to make square
parcels.

Heat remaining butter in a wok and
carefully slide in the parcels. Fry over a
high heat until they are golden brown on
both sides. Turn them out and cut each
parcel into quarters. Serve warm,
sprinkled with caster sugar.

Makes 4 pancakes

SILVER PIN NOODLES WITH SHREDDED CHICKEN

NOODLES

1 cup wheat starch (125 g)
pinch salt
¾ cup boiling water (180 mL)
2 teaspoons oil

CHICKEN MIXTURE

1 chicken thigh fillet, sliced
½ teaspoon chopped fresh ginger root
½ teaspoon Chinese white wine or
   ordinary white wine
1 teaspoon cornflour
oil, for frying
1 Chinese mushroom, soaked in warm
   water for 20 minutes
1 shallot, chopped
1 clove garlic
1 green capsicum, seeded and sliced
1 red capsicum, seeded and sliced
120 g bean sprouts

*Silver Pin Noodles with Shredded
Chicken (above) and Beef and Shallot
Fried Rice (below)*

SEASONINGS

2 teaspoons oyster sauce
1 teaspoon sugar
2 teaspoons soy sauce
¼ teaspoon sesame oil

Sift wheat starch and salt in a mixing bowl. Pour in boiling water and stir. Cover for 5 minutes then remove and knead to form a smooth dough.

Roll out into a long sausage-shaped roll and cut into 24 equal portions. Knead each portion into the shape of a thin chopstick and cut again into 5 cm portions. Pinch ends to make them pointed. Put silver pin noodles on a greased plate to steam for 5 minutes. When cooked, coat with oil to prevent them from sticking together.

Marinate chicken for 20 minutes with ginger, Chinese white wine and cornflour. Shallow-fry in hot oil 5 minutes and set aside. Steam mushrooms, chop and set aside.

Heat pan and add more oil. Saute briefly shallot, garlic and capsicum then bean sprouts. Add chicken meat, silver pin noodles and mushrooms. Saute together a few minutes, sprinkle with wine, add seasonings and serve hot.

Serves 4–6

SAGO PUDDING

235 g sago
2 cups sugar (500 g)
125 g butter
1 cup milk (250 mL)
2 cups coconut milk (500 mL) (see Note)
1 cup cornflour (125 g)
½ cup custard powder (125 g)
4 eggs, well beaten

Soak sago well in water 3 hours. Pour sago into a pan of boiling water and simmer until transparent. Wash under running tap. Drain and set aside.

Put 1 litre water and the sugar into a saucepan. Slowly bring to the boil and add sago, butter and milk stirring until well blended.

Mix coconut milk with cornflour and custard powder. Gradually stir into boiling sugar mixture. Continue stirring until thickened. Remove from heat.

Add well-beaten eggs and stir until smooth. Pour into a heatproof container and place on middle shelf of preheated oven 230°C (450°F). Bake for 25 minutes or until golden brown.

Note: Coconut milk can be replaced by half water and half ordinary milk.

Serves 10–15

BEEF AND SHALLOT FRIED RICE

20 g butter
450 g skirt steak, cut into very small
   dice
2 cups cold cooked rice (400 g)
salt and pepper
3 teaspoons soy sauce
2 teaspoons sugar
pinch pepper
3 shallots, very finely chopped

Melt butter in a wok and stir-fry steak until it has changed colour. Add rice and stir-fry over a high heat until rice is heated through. Add seasoning and serve decorated with finely chopped shallots.

Note: For better results, cook rice the day before, or use leftover rice. Cook as quickly as possible, without burning.

Serves 4–6

PORK AND LETTUCE ROLLS

30 g dried Chinese mushrooms, soaked
 in warm water 20 minutes
45 g water chestnuts
60 g bamboo shoots
3 shallots
200 g canned crab
2 teaspoons oil
125 g minced pork
1 teaspoon sesame oil
2 teaspoons soy sauce
1 teaspoon oyster sauce
1 tablespoon sherry
1 lettuce, washed and dried

Drain mushrooms, remove stems and
chop mushroom caps finely. Very finely
chop water chestnuts, bamboo shoots
and shallots. Drain and flake crab.

Heat oil in a wok and stir-fry pork until
golden. Stir in mushrooms, water chestnuts, bamboo shoots, shallots and crab.
Cook 1 minute. Combine sesame oil, soy
sauce, oyster sauce and sherry and stir
into the mixture.

Place 2 level tablespoons of the mixture into the centre of each lettuce leaf.
Fold in the ends of the lettuce leaf and
roll up to form a neat parcel.

Generally, meat filling and lettuce
leaves are served separately, guests fill
and roll their own lettuce leaves.

Serves 4

VANILLA SPONGE

1 cup plain flour (125 g)
½ cup custard powder (125 g)
2 teaspoons baking powder
½ teaspoon bicarbonate of soda
6 eggs
1 ½ cups sugar (375 g)
½ teaspoon vanilla essence
125 g butter
almonds or olive kernels

Sift flour, custard powder, baking powder
and bicarbonate of soda together three
times, then set aside.

Beat eggs in a bowl, add sugar gradually and continue beating until mixture is
light and fluffy. Fold dry ingredients into
the egg mixture. Add vanilla essence and
set aside for 30 minutes. In a pan, melt
butter and gradually add the batter.

Line one 18 cm square tin with two
pieces of greased paper then put into a
steamer. Pour in batter and steam for
about 50 minutes or until cooked.
Arrange almonds for decoration. Cut
cake into 16 square pieces and serve.

Note: This cake is best eaten hot. Olive
kernels are only available from Asian
foodstores.

Pork and Lettuce Rolls

SAVOURY SOUPS

Soup is an integral part of the Chinese banquet, or smorgasboard style of serving a variety of dishes at the one meal. Enjoy the original Chicken Noodle Soup, try wonderful Peking Hot Sour Soup, or a children's favourite, Crab and Sweet Corn Soup.

SHORT SOUP

24 wonton skins
1 egg white, beaten
1 litre boiling salted water
1.5 litres boiling chicken stock
2 shallots, finely chopped

FILLING

250 g pork, minced
250 g prawn meat, chopped
2 shallots, finely chopped
1 egg, beaten
¼ teaspoon salt
2 teaspoons soy sauce
½ teaspoon sugar
½ teaspoon sesame oil

Mix all filling ingredients together. Place a teaspoon of filling onto a wonton skin. Moisten edges with egg white. Fold skin in half to form a triangle, pressing edges to seal. Fold the corners of the long edge together and fasten with egg white. Repeat until all wonton skins are filled.

Drop dumplings into boiling salted water and cook for 5 minutes; drain.

Place four dumplings into each bowl. Cover with boiling stock and sprinkle with shallots.

Serves 6

FISH AND SPINACH SOUP

250 g firm white fish fillets, cut in
    2 cm × 1 cm slices
2 tablespoons seasoned cornflour
1.5 litres fish stock
1 ½ tablespoons light soy sauce
1 tablespoon ginger wine
300 g spinach leaf, cut in 2 cm pieces
salt and pepper

Toss fish slices in cornflour to coat.

Bring stock to the boil. Add soy sauce, wine and fish pieces. Simmer covered for 6 minutes. Add spinach, cook uncovered until bright green, 1–2 minutes. Adjust seasonings and serve.

Serves 6

CHICKEN NOODLE SOUP

250 g thin long life noodles
1 tablespoon light soy sauce
¼ teaspoon sesame oil
250 g chicken breast, cooked and cut
    in 5 cm strips
½ bunch fresh mustard cabbage, cut
    in 2 cm pieces (see Glossary)
2 litres chicken stock

Cook noodles in 1 litre boiling salted water for 5 minutes; drain.

Place soy sauce and sesame oil in a large soup bowl. Top with cooked noodles. Arrange chicken and cabbage on top. Pour over boiling seasoned stock. Cover and let stand a few minutes before serving.

Serves 6–8

GARNISHES FOR SOUP

Both shredded ham and egg are frequently used to garnish soups and other dishes.

HAM GARNISH

Cut a thick slice of ham into shreds. The pieces are usually placed in the centre rather than being scattered over the top of the dish.

EGG GARNISH

Beat 1 egg briefly. Heat 1 teaspoon oil in a wok. Add egg and tilt the wok to form a layer of egg. Cook egg until set, roll up Swiss-roll style, and cut into slices. As with the ham garnish, the strips of egg are placed in the centre of the dish. Both ham and egg garnish may be diced.

Clockwise from left to right: Chicken Noodle Soup, Short Soup and Fish and Spinach Soup

PORK BALL AND VERMICELLI SOUP

125 g vermicelli noodles
1.5 litres pork stock or canned
  consomme
250 g frozen pork balls (available in
  packets at Asian foodstores)
1–2 tablespoons light soy sauce
salt and pepper
1 shallot, finely chopped

Cut vermicelli with scissors into 5 cm lengths. Cover with boiling water, let stand 5 minutes then drain.

Bring stock to the boil. Add pork balls and simmer for 5 minutes. Add vermicelli and soy sauce, and simmer covered for 5 minutes. Adjust seasoning and serve, garnish with shallot.

Serves 6

ASPARAGUS EGG FLOWER SOUP

1.5 litres chicken stock
340 g canned asparagus cuts,
  reserving canned liquid
200 g chicken, steamed and shredded
salt and pepper
1 tablespoon cornflour blended with
2 tablespoons stock
2 eggs, lightly beaten
1 shallot, finely chopped

Heat stock. Add asparagus and liquid. When boiling, add shredded chicken and season to taste.

Blend cornflour mixture into soup, stirring to thicken. When boiling, remove from heat. Pour in egg slowly. Garnish with shallot.

Serves 6–8

SHARK'S FIN SOUP

2 litres chicken stock
425 g canned shark's fin
200 g chicken, steamed and finely
  chopped
2 teaspoons light soy sauce
2 teaspoons dry sherry
salt and pepper
2 teaspoons cornflour
1 tablespoon water
1 egg, lightly beaten
60 g minced ham
2 shallots, finely chopped

Bring chicken stock to the boil. Add shark's fin and return to the boil. Add chopped cooked chicken. Combine soy sauce, sherry, salt, pepper, cornflour and water. Stir into soup. Simmer 5 minutes. Remove soup from heat. Pour in egg slowly, which will cook and rise to the surface. Pour soup into serving bowl. Garnish with ham and shallots.

Serves 8

CRAB AND SWEET CORN SOUP

1 tablespoon vegetable oil
½ teaspoon chopped fresh ginger root
1.5 litres fish stock, seasoned
1 tablespoon dry sherry
220 g crabmeat, flaked
125 g sweet corn
1 tablespoon cornflour blended with
  2 tablespoons stock or water
2 egg whites, lightly beaten
chopped shallots, to garnish

Heat oil in a wok. Add ginger and crabmeat, stir-fry 2 minutes. Add stock, sherry and sweet corn. When boiling, stir in blended cornflour and water to thicken. Remove from heat.

Pour in egg white in a thin stream. Garnish with shallots.

Note: Children often love this soup when it is adapted to use chicken instead of crab. Simply substitute an equal quantity of chicken stock for fish stock, and chicken for crabmeat.

Serves 6–8

Crab and Sweet Corn Soup

Peking Hot Sour Soup

BEAN CURD AND VEGETABLE SOUP

1.5 litres vegetable stock
1 ripe tomato, skinned, seeded and cut
  in 1 cm dice
5 button mushrooms, sliced
60 g bean sprouts, root removed
125 g bean curd, sliced
salt and pepper
1 shallot, finely chopped

Bring stock to the boil. Add tomato and mushrooms and simmer for 3 minutes. Add sprouts, bean curd and seasonings. Simmer covered for 2 minutes. Garnish with shallot.

Serves 6

PEKING HOT SOUR SOUP

4 Chinese mushrooms, soaked in warm
  water 20 minutes
1 litre chicken stock
125 g lean pork, shredded
60 g canned bamboo shoots,
  shredded
125 g bean curd, cut in 1 cm dice
2 tablespoons white vinegar
1 tablespoon soy sauce
1 tablespoon cornflour blended with
  4 tablespoons water
1 egg, beaten
½ teaspoon sesame oil
3 shallots, chopped

Squeeze mushrooms dry and remove stems. Cut mushroom caps into thin strips.

Bring stock to the boil and add pork and mushrooms. Bring to the boil again, reduce heat and simmer for 8–10 minutes. Add bamboo shoots and bean curd and simmer for another 4–5 minutes.

Mix vinegar and soy sauce and stir into soup. Stir in blended cornflour and water and simmer, stirring constantly, until thickened.

Stir in beaten egg off the heat. Add sesame oil and shallots and serve hot.

Serves 4–6

To fold wontons: place ½ teaspoon of filling in wrapper, fold in half and press sides together; fold in half again, pressing firmly at both sides of filling, but leaving corners open.

Bring two corners together, and cross over in front of filling; where they meet, brush lightly with water or beaten egg, to make them stick.

Wonton Soup

WONTON SOUP

WONTONS

2 Chinese mushrooms, soaked in warm
　water 20 minutes
90 g lean minced pork
60 g prawn meat, minced
2 water chestnuts, very finely chopped
4 shallots, very finely chopped
1 tablespoon soy sauce
2 teaspoons sherry
16 wonton wrappers
1 egg, lightly beaten

SOUP

1.5 litres chicken stock
6 shallots, white part only, thinly sliced
1 quantity Egg Garnish (see recipe)

Squeeze mushrooms dry. Remove stalks and finely chop the caps. Combine mushrooms, pork, prawns, water chestnuts, shallots, soy sauce and sherry. Stand 30 minutes.

Place ½ teaspoon of filling slightly off centre of each wrapper. Fold wrapper in half and press the edges together to seal them. Again, fold the wrapper in half. Pull the corners down into a crescent shape, overlapping the corners. Seal the overlap with a little beaten egg.

Drop the wontons one by one into boiling salted water and simmer 7 minutes, making sure they do not stick to the bottom of the pan. Drain the wontons. Bring chicken stock to the boil and add wontons and shallots. Top each serving with a little Egg Garnish.

Serves 6–8

ABALONE AND PORK SOUP

2 tablespoons oil
125 g lean pork, cut in 2.5 cm dice
125 g canned abalone, cut in 2.5 cm
　dice, reserve liquid
1 litre chicken stock
2 tablespoons dry sherry
2 tablespoons soy sauce
1 teaspoon shredded fresh ginger root
60 g canned bamboo shoot, diced
1 shallot, to garnish
chilli sauce (optional)

Heat oil in a saucepan, add pork and abalone and cook over high heat until meat changes colour. Drain, discarding any excess oil.

Combine reserved abalone liquid, stock, sherry and soy sauce and bring to the boil. Add ginger and bamboo shoot, reduce heat and simmer for 2 minutes. Add pork and abalone and heat through. Slice shallot to form flower shapes, for garnish. Serve hot with chilli sauce separately if liked.

Serves 4

Pork and Prawn Soup

CREAM OF CRAB SOUP

1.5 litres fish stock
125 g crabmeat
1 tablespoon dry sherry
1 tablespoon cornflour blended with
  2 tablespoons stock or water
salt and pepper
½ teaspoon sesame oil
2 egg whites
3 tablespoons cream
1 shallot, finely chopped

Bring stock to the boil. Add crabmeat, sherry and blended cornflour and stock. Simmer 3 minutes. Add seasonings and sesame oil.

Beat egg whites until frothy, then fold in cream. Lightly stir into soup and remove from heat. Garnish with shallot.

Serves 6–8

PORK AND PRAWN SOUP

350 g egg noodles
3 tablespoons oil
1 small onion, thinly sliced
2 slices fresh ginger root, finely
  chopped
250 g lean pork, finely shredded
50 g Chinese mushrooms, soaked in
  warm water 20 minutes and shredded
½ Chinese cabbage, shredded and
  blanched
100 g bean sprouts
125 g prawns
2 tablespoons soy sauce
1 litre beef or chicken stock

Cook noodles as directed.

Heat oil in a wok. Add onion, ginger and pork and stir-fry for 2 minutes.

Add mushrooms, cabbage, bean sprouts and prawns; stir-fry for 2 minutes. Stir in soy sauce and stir-fry a further 1½ minutes. Remove from heat and keep warm.

Bring stock to the boil. Add half the pork mixture and bring to the boil again. Add noodles and heat through. Serve soup and top with remaining hot pork mixture.

Serves 6

Seafood Sensations

Almond Prawn Cutlets, Sizzling Mongolian Scallops, Stir-fried Crab, Ginger and Shallots — anyone looking for spectacular alternatives to red meat will find something special here. Whether for nutritious meals, light snacks or as part of an impressive Chinese banquet, these dishes are low on kilojoules and great on taste.

COMBINATION SEAFOOD IN NESTS

3 tablespoons vegetable oil
½ teaspoon salt
½ teaspoon chopped fresh ginger root
125 g scallops
125 g prepared squid cut into rings (see box on Squid Preparation)
125 g green (uncooked) prawns, shelled and deveined
125 g firm white fish, cut in 2.5 cm dice
½ teaspoon chopped garlic
125 g broccoli florets
125 g snow peas, stems removed
60 g Chinese cabbage, stems cut in 3 cm × 1 cm pieces
30 g bamboo shoots, sliced
30 g mini corn
15 g champignons, sliced
15 g straw mushrooms
1 tablespoon light soy sauce
2 tablespoons dry sherry
1 teaspoon sugar
pinch pepper
½ cup fish stock (125 mL)
2 tablespoons oyster sauce
1 tablespoon cornflour
3 tablespoons water or stock
noodle nests (see recipes)

Heat half the oil. Add salt and ginger, and stir-fry 30 seconds. Add seafood and cook 2 minutes. Remove from pan.

Heat remaining oil, add garlic, broccoli, snow peas and cabbage stems. Stir-fry 2 minutes. Add bamboo shoots, corn, champignons and straw mushrooms. Blend in soy sauce, sherry, sugar, pepper and stock.

Blend oyster sauce, cornflour and water. Bring sauce to the boil, and stir in cornflour mixture to thicken. Fold in seafood to reheat. Serve in noodle nests — see recipes for Vermicelli Nests or Fresh Egg Noodle Baskets.

SIZZLING MONGOLIAN SCALLOPS

500 g scallops
1 tablespoon light soy sauce
1 tablespoon dry sherry
2 tablespoons vegetable oil
1 large onion, cut in eighths
1 teaspoon chopped fresh ginger root

SAUCE

1 teaspoon chilli garlic sauce
2 teaspoons hoisin sauce
1 teaspoon sesame oil
½ teaspoon five spice powder
1 teaspoon sugar
3 teaspoons peanut butter
3 tablespoons fish stock

For this recipe you will need one sizzle plate, which consists of an iron plate that fits into a thick wooden mould of similar shape. Heat the iron plate on top of your stove for 5 minutes before adding cooked ingredients. In a bowl combine scallops, soy sauce and sherry. Heat oil in a wok. Add onion and stir-fry 1 minute. Add ginger, scallops and marinade, stir-fry 2–3 minutes. Blend in sauce ingredients and stir-fry until boiling. Serve at once on hot sizzle plate.

Serves 6

SQUID PREPARATION

To prepare squid, remove the outer purple membrane. Place knife into tube and cut through at one edge. Open out tube. Lightly cut the inner surface to form a small diamond pattern. This acts as a tenderiser and enables the squid strips to curl when being stir-fried. Cut squid into 4 cm × 2 cm strips for cooking.

Sizzling Mongolian Scallops (above) and Combination Seafood in Nests (below)

FISH COCKTAILS WITH CHINESE PICKLE SAUCE

500 g firm white fish fillets
seasoned cornflour

BATTER

1 cup plain flour (125 g)
½ teaspoon salt
2 eggs, beaten
½ cup milk (125 mL)
½ cup water (125 mL)
2 teaspoons vegetable oil

SAUCE

2 teaspoons tomato sauce
¼ teaspoon salt
2 teaspoons soy sauce
2 cups unsweetened pineapple juice
   (500 mL)
180 g Chinese mixed pickles, sliced
50 g pineapple pieces
½ capsicum, cut in 1 cm dice
2 tablespoons vinegar
2 tablespoons cornflour

Cut fish into 2 cm cubes and roll in cornflour. To make batter, sift flour and salt in a bowl, add eggs, milk, water, and oil and combine well to form a batter. Dip fish cubes in batter and deep-fry in hot oil until golden.

To make sauce, combine ingredients in saucepan. Stir until boiling. Spoon sauce over seafood and serve at once.

Serves 4–6

CRABMEAT SAUCE OVER BROCCOLI

1 tablespoon vegetable oil
1 slice fresh ginger root
1 clove garlic, crushed
750 g broccoli florets
¼ teaspoon salt
1 teaspoon light soy sauce
½ teaspoon sugar
2 tablespoons dry sherry
3 tablespoons fish stock or water
250 g crabmeat; fresh, frozen or
   canned
1 tablespoon shredded red capsicum,
   blanched

SAUCE

1 tablespoon dry sherry or white wine
¼ teaspoon salt
pinch pepper
1 cup fish stock (250 mL)
1 tablespoon cornflour blended with
2 tablespoons stock or water

Heat oil in a wok. Add ginger and garlic and cook until golden; remove. Add broccoli, stirring to coat with oil. Stir in salt, soy sauce, sugar, sherry and stock. Cook covered for 3–4 minutes until broccoli is bright green. Avoid overcooking.

Remove to serving platter and keep warm.

To make sauce heat sherry, salt, pepper and stock. Stir in blended cornflour and stock to thicken. When boiling, stir in crabmeat. Simmer 2–3 minutes. Pour sauce over broccoli, garnish with capsicum and serve.

Serves 4–6

PRAWNS CHOW MEIN

10 Chinese mushrooms, soaked in warm
   water 20 minutes
2 tablespoons oil
2 stalks celery, sliced
125 g bamboo shoots, sliced
250 g bean sprouts, washed
250 g water chestnuts, drained and
   sliced
½ cup chicken stock (125 mL)
1 tablespoon dry sherry
1 tablespoon soy sauce
500 g school prawns, shelled

Drain mushrooms, squeeze dry and discard stalks. Slice caps into strips. Heat oil in a wok. Add celery, bamboo shoots, mushrooms, bean sprouts and water chestnuts. Stir-fry about 2 minutes until vegetables are tender but crisp.

Pour in stock and sherry. Increase to high and bring to the boil. Reduce heat and stir in soy sauce and prawns. Cover and cook for 3 minutes. Remove from heat and serve immediately.

Serves 4

Prawns Chow Mein

ALMOND PRAWN CUTLETS

750 g green (uncooked) king prawns,
  shelled and deveined retaining tail
1 ½ cups vegetable oil (375 mL)
1 slice green fresh ginger root
prawn crisps, various colours
½ cup plain flour (60 g)
¼ teaspoon salt
1 egg, separated
½ cup water (125 mL)
3 tablespoons seasoned cornflour
125 g almonds, chopped
1 lemon cut in eighths

Cut each prawn lengthways, halfway
through from deveined side. Place cut
side down and press gently with hand to
form a butterfly-shaped cutlet.

Heat oil in a wok. Add ginger, when
brown remove. Add 4 prawn crisps at a
time. They will puff up and double in size.
Remove immediately to avoid browning.
Drain on absorbent kitchen paper.

Sieve flour and salt into a basin. Beat in
egg yolk and water to form a batter. Fold
in beaten egg white.

Dust prawns with cornflour, dip into
batter. Drain off excess and sprinkle with
chopped almonds.

Reheat oil, deep-fry prawns until tail
turns pink, about 3 minutes. Serve garnished with prawn crisps and lemon
wedges.

Serves 4–6

FISH SLICES IN HONEY SAUCE

500 g firm white fish fillets
2 tablespoons cornflour seasoned with
  salt and pepper
1 cup plain flour (125 g)
1 ¼ cups cold water (310 mL)
1 egg, beaten
1 ½ cups vegetable oil (375 mL)
2 slices fresh ginger root
1 tablespoon vegetable oil
2 tablespoons honey
1 tablespoon toasted sesame seeds

Cut fish fillets in half lengthways. Remove
any bones. Cut diagonally into strips
2 cm x 4 cm. Dust with some cornflour
just before frying.

Sieve seasoned cornflour and plain
flour into a basin. Blend in water and egg
to form batter. Strain and set aside.

Heat oil with ginger in a wok. When ginger turns golden remove from oil.

Shake excess flour from fish. Dip into
batter. Fry in small batches until golden.
Drain well on absorbent kitchen paper.
Keep warm on serving plate.

Heat remaining oil, blend in honey.
When hot pour over fish and sprinkle with
sesame seeds.

Serves 6

STIR-FRIED CRAB, GINGER AND SHALLOTS

2 large live crabs
2 tablespoons oil
1 clove garlic, crushed
3 thin slices fresh ginger root, finely
  chopped
1 bunch shallots, sliced
¾ cup chicken stock (180 mL)
1 tablespoon soy sauce
1 tablespoon sherry
¼ teaspoon sugar
dash sesame oil
2 teaspoons cornflour blended with
2 tablespoons water

Cut green crabs in half and segment
them. Heat oil in a wok. Add garlic, ginger
and shallots, and stir-fry for 30 seconds.
Add crab pieces and stir-fry to coat with
oil. Pour in stock, soy sauce, sherry,
sugar and sesame oil and bring quickly to
the boil.

Cook covered until crab shells turn
pink. Stir in blended cornflour, bring to
the boil and serve.

Serves 4

Segment crab with a cleaver.

Stir-fry crab in a wok with oil, garlic,
ginger and shallots.

Stir-fried Crab, Ginger and Shallots

SIMMERED WHOLE FISH

1 kg whole fish
1.5 litres water
2 shallots, cut in large pieces
2 thin slices fresh green ginger root,
    finely chopped
2 tablespoons sherry
1 tablespoon soy sauce
4 tablespoons oil
4 shallots, sliced finely
2 slices red ginger, finely sliced
2 tablespoons soy sauce
1 teaspoon sesame oil

Clean and scale fish, leaving head and tail intact. Score, rinse under cold running water and drain.

Bring water to the boil. Add shallots, ginger, sherry, soy sauce and 2 tablespoons oil to the water, and return to boil.

Place fish on a skimmer and lower into the boiling liquid. Reduce heat, cover and simmer gently 5 minutes. Turn off heat completely and leave, covered, for 20–25 minutes. Remove the fish carefully onto a serving platter. Sprinkle over finely sliced shallots, red ginger and soy sauce. Heat remaining 2 tablespoons oil with sesame oil until sizzling, and pour over fish.

Serves 4

SIZZLING SQUID IN SPECIAL SAUCE

500 g prepared squid (see box on Squid
    Preparation)
1½ cups vegetable oil for deep frying
    (375 mL)
1 teaspoon chopped garlic
½ teaspoon chopped fresh ginger root
2 shallots, cut into 3 cm lengths
2 teaspoons brown sugar
1½ tablespoons white wine
2 tablespoons soy sauce
1 tablespoon hoisin sauce
½ teaspoon chilli sauce

Heat most of the oil in a pan. Deep-fry squid 1 minute. Remove and drain.

Reheat 1½ tablespoons oil. Add garlic, ginger, shallots and stir-fry. Add sugar, wine, soy, hoisin and chilli sauces. Stir in squid to reheat, and coat with sauce. Place onto hot sizzle plate to serve.

Serves 4–6

STIR-FRIED SQUID AND VEGETABLES

700 g squid
3 Chinese mushrooms soaked in warm
    water 20 minutes
1 bunch Chinese spinach or cabbage
3 tablespoons oil
1 onion
¼ teaspoon grated fresh ginger root
60 g bamboo shoots
100 g carrot, finely sliced
100 g green beans, finely chopped
100 g capsicum, finely sliced
½ cup chicken stock (125 mL)
1 tablespoon soy sauce
2 teaspoons cornflour blended with
1 tablespoon water

Pull tentacles and intestines out of squid. Pull 'feather' out of body and discard. Cut tentacles from intestines, discard intestines. Rinse body and tentacles and peel skin from body. Drain well. Halve bodies lengthways and score the surface.

Discard mushroom stalks and slice caps.

Cut spinach into 5 cm strips. Parboil stalks for 3 minutes, drain and refresh under cold running water. Halve onion lengthways then cut into 4 lengthways strips. Separate into layers. Slice bamboo shoots.

Heat oil in a wok. Stir-fry prepared squid 1 minute. Add onion and stir-fry for 30 seconds.

Add ginger, spinach, mushrooms, bamboo shoots, carrot, beans and capsicum and stir-fry a further 30 seconds. Pour in chicken stock and soy sauce. Bring to the boil, reduce heat and simmer, covered, 3 minutes.

Stir blended cornflour and water into sauce and cook until thickened. Serve hot with steamed rice.

Serves 4

HONEYED PRAWNS

2 tablespoons oil
1 clove garlic, crushed
1 slice fresh ginger root, finely chopped
750 g green (uncooked) prawns, shelled
    with tail intact
¼ cup honey (80 g)
2 teaspoons soy sauce
sesame seeds

Heat oil in a wok. Add garlic and ginger and stir-fry for 30 seconds. Add prawns in two batches and stir-fry until pink. Remove the first batch before cooking the second. Pour over combined honey and soy sauce, toss quickly.

Serve sprinkled with sesame seeds.

Serves 4

WHOLE FISH IN BLACK BEAN SAUCE

750 g whole fish, cleaned and scaled
    (fish cutlets or fillets can also be used)
½ teaspoon salt
1 tablespoon plain flour
½ cup vegetable oil (125 mL)
½ teaspoon chopped fresh ginger root
½ teaspoon chopped garlic
1 tablespoon black beans, chopped
2 teaspoons dry sherry
2 teaspoons soy sauce
½ teaspoon sugar
1 cup fish stock or water (250 mL)
2 teaspoons cornflour blended with 1
    tablespoon water
2 medium shallots, chopped
1 tablespoon shredded red capsicum,
    blanched 1 minute in boiling water

Score fish on both sides. Season lightly with salt, then coat with flour.

Heat oil in a pan. Add fish and fry on both sides until golden. Remove to serving plate and keep hot. Pour off excess oil from pan leaving 1 tablespoon. Reheat, add ginger, garlic and beans, stir-fry 1 minute. Stir in sherry, soy sauce, sugar and stock. When boiling, stir in blended cornflour and water to thicken.

Add shallots. Spoon over fish and garnish with capsicum.

Serves 6

Right: How to shell prawns and remove veins with the point of a knife.
Below: Whole Fish in Black Bean Sauce

Butterfly Prawns

BUTTERFLY PRAWNS

4 tablespoons plain flour
½ teaspoon salt
1 egg, beaten
4 tablespoons beer or water
12 green (uncooked) king prawns
12 bacon strips cut 1 cm x 5 cm
24 small broccoli florets, blanched
2 tablespoons seasoned cornflour
1 ½ cups vegetable oil, for deep-
    frying (375 mL)
lemon wedges, to serve

Sieve flour and salt. Stir in egg and beer
to form batter. Cut prawns through centre
lengthways to the tail.

Shell and devein prawns, retaining tail.
Wrap one strip of bacon around tail end
of each prawn. Insert toothpicks to
fasten. Place one broccoli floret onto
each side of toothpick. Wrap each half of
prawn around broccoli and fasten onto
toothpick. Sprinkle prawns with cornflour.
Lightly coat with batter. Do not batter the
tail.

Heat oil. Fry prawns one at a time until
tail turns pink, 2–3 minutes. Drain well.
Serve with lemon and dip sauce of your
own choice.

Serves 2

CRAB FOO YUNG

4 eggs
1 teaspoon soy sauce
½ teaspoon chilli sauce
2 teaspoons sherry
250 g fresh or canned crabmeat
3 tablespoons oil
6 Chinese mushrooms, soaked in
   warm water 20 minutes
6 shallots, finely diced

SAUCE

1 cup chicken stock (250 mL)
2 teaspoons soy sauce
1 tablespoon cornflour blended with
1 tablespoon water

Beat eggs lightly in a bowl. Stir in soy and chilli sauces with sherry. Shred crabmeat.

Heat 1 tablespoon oil in a wok. Discard mushroom stalks and slice caps. Stir-fry mushrooms and shallots for 2 minutes; add crabmeat and stir-fry 1 minute over high heat.

Remove wok from heat. Remove the mixture to a bowl, cool a few minutes and combine with egg mixture.

Heat 2 tablespoons oil in wok. Add a quarter of mixture and cook until the omelette is just set and lightly browned on the underside. Turn and cook for 1 minute. Place omelette on a serving plate. Repeat to make a total of 4 omelettes. Serve with sauce.

To make sauce, bring stock, soy sauce and blended cornflour and water to the boil, stirring constantly. Simmer 1 minute.

Serves 2

FISH BALLS

1 kg firm white, unfrozen fish fillets
2 eggs
1 tablespoon ginger wine
2 teaspoons cornflour
½ teaspoon salt
pinch white pepper
stock or water

Cut fish into 2 cm cubes. Blend in a food processor with remaining ingredients. Shape mixture into 2 cm balls, with wet hands. Add balls to boiling stock or water to cover. Cook over medium heat 4 minutes, drain.

Once cooked, fish balls will keep refrigerated for several days. Use in soups, add to stir-fried seafood combinations or deep-fry and serve with various sauces.

Makes approximately 20

CRUMBED KING PRAWN CUTLETS

12 green (uncooked) king prawns
2 eggs, beaten
1 tablespoon dry sherry
3 tablespoons seasoned cornflour
fine dry bread crumbs
1½ cups vegetable oil (375 mL)
1 lemon cut in eighths

PLUM SAUCE DIP

3 tablespoons plum sauce
2 teaspoons ginger wine

Shell and devein prawns, leaving tail intact. Cut each prawn lengthways halfway through from deveined side. Place cut side down and press gently with hand to form a butterfly-shaped cutlet.

Combine eggs with sherry. Coat prawns with cornflour, shaking off excess flour. Dip into egg then coat evenly with breadcrumbs.

Deep-fry in hot oil 3 minutes until golden. Drain on absorbent kitchen paper. Serve hot with plum sauce dip and lemon wedges.

To make dip warm plum sauce, stir in wine and serve in dip sauce bowl.

Serves 6

Crab Foo Yung

Stir-fried Lobster and Pork
Chop lobster in half with a cleaver.

Stir-fry lobster until shell is red and flesh is white.

Stir-fried Lobster and Pork

Stir-fry pork mixture until meat turns brown.

PRAWN AND HAM TOAST

6 slices day-old white bread, each cut
  into 4 rounds
oil, for shallow-frying
2 thin slices of ham, finely chopped

TOPPING

250 g green (uncooked) prawns,
  chopped
2 tablespoons grated water chestnuts
1 egg, beaten
1½ teaspoons cornflour
1 teaspoon ginger wine
1 teaspoon light soy sauce
¼ teaspoon salt
pinch white pepper

Combine topping ingredients. Spread mixture evenly over bread rounds with a wet-bladed knife. Sprinkle with chopped ham and press gently into topping.

Heat 2–3 cm of oil in a pan. Place round in oil, prawn-side down. Fry 1½ minutes. Turn rounds over and fry until golden. Drain and serve hot.

Serves 2–4

STIR-FRIED LOBSTER AND PORK

1 kg green (uncooked) lobster
3 tablespoons oil
1 clove garlic, crushed
1 thin slice fresh ginger root, finely
  chopped
2 tablespoons soy sauce
1 tablespoon sherry
¼ teaspoon sesame oil
175 g lean pork, minced
4 tablespoons chicken stock
1 egg, beaten

Place lobster on its back on a chopping board. Chop with a heavy cleaver down its entire length. Chop tail into 5 cm pieces. Cut legs in half and chop each claw into 3 pieces.

Heat oil in a wok. Stir in garlic and ginger. Add lobster and stir-fry for 2½ minutes until shell is bright red and lobster meat is white and opaque. Remove lobster.

Combine soy sauce, sherry, sesame oil and pork. Stir-fry for 2 minutes or until pork has lost any trace of pink. Return lobster to wok.

Add chicken stock and heat to boiling point. Stir in egg and stir-fry 30 seconds.

Serves 4

DEEP-FRIED WHOLE FISH AND VEGETABLES IN SWEET AND SOUR SAUCE

1 kg whole fish, cleaned and scaled
1 ½ cups Sweet and Sour Sauce
  (375mL) see recipe
2 carrots, sliced diagonally
2 tablespoons oil
1 clove garlic, crushed
2 thin slices fresh green ginger root,
  grated
1 medium onion, cut into wedges
1 small green capsicum, cut into strips
4 fresh mushrooms, sliced
125 g bamboo shoots, shredded
oil for deep frying
1 egg, beaten
cornflour

Bone fish leaving sides attached at tail. Score fish lightly on both sides. Prepare the sauce but do not thicken. Parboil carrots in water for 4–5 minutes, and cool under cold running water.

Heat oil in a wok. Add garlic and ginger, and stir-fry for 1 minute. Discard garlic and ginger. Add onion, capsicum, carrots, mushrooms and bamboo shoots to wok and stir-fry 2–3 minutes. Stir in sauce, cover and cook for 1½ minutes. Remove from heat.

Heat oil for deep-frying. Brush fish, inside and out, with beaten egg and dredge with cornflour. Deep-fry fish for about 6 minutes or until golden brown and tender. Remove fish with a skimmer and drain on paper towels.

Bring sauce to the boil and stir in blended cornflour to thicken. Place fish on a serving dish and pour over sauce.

Serves 4–6

BRAISED ABALONE WITH CHINESE CABBAGE

1 tablespoon vegetable oil
1 teaspoon fresh chopped ginger root
½ teaspoon chopped garlic
500 g choy sum cabbage, cut into 5 cm
  lengths
1 teaspoon sugar
2 teaspoons dry sherry
½ cup reserved canned abalone liquid
  (125 mL)
1 teaspoon sesame oil
1 tablespoon oyster sauce
1 tablespoon soy sauce
2 teaspoons cornflour
600 g canned abalone, thinly sliced —
  retain liquid
3 tablespoons water

Heat oil. Add ginger, garlic and cabbage stems. Stir-fry 1 minute. Add cabbage leaf, sugar, sherry and abalone liquid. Cook until vegetable is bright green. Arrange cabbage on serving platter and keep warm.

Add sesame oil, oyster and soy sauces to pan. Blend cornflour with remaining liquid. Stir into thicken when boiling. Reduce heat, and fold in abalone slices, to heat through briefly. Extended cooking will toughen abalone. Arrange slices over cabbage. Spoon over sauce and serve at once.

Serves 6–8

Braised Abalone with Chinese Cabbage

SET THE PACE WITH PORK

Pork is popular — the Chinese love its versatility. Everyone knows Sweet and Sour Pork; why not treat the family to Pineapple Pork, Deep-fried Szechuan Pork, or a stunning dinner party centrepiece, Crisp Roast Belly of Pork?

BRAISED PORK FILLET IN PEKING SAUCE

400 g pork fillets, thinly sliced
1 teaspoon cornflour
1 tablespoon soy sauce
1 tablespoon dry sherry
1 tablespoon stock
350 g Chinese spinach, blanched in
    boiling stock for 1 minute
2 tablespoons vegetable oil
2 tablespoons hoisin sauce
½ teaspoon sesame oil or seeds

Combine pork with cornflour, soy sauce, sherry and stock. Let stand 15 minutes. Puree spinach, arrange on a serving platter and keep warm.

Heat oil in a wok. Stir-fry pork until it changes colour, 2–3 minutes. Remove from oil.

Reheat oil, add hoisin sauce. When hot, return pork. Stir-fry to reheat and coat with sauce. Add sesame oil. Serve over spinach.

Serves 4–6

PINEAPPLE PORK

2 tablespoons vegetable oil
1 teaspoon chopped garlic
500 g lean pork, cut in 1 cm dice
1 onion, cut in 1 cm dice
½ teaspoon salt
1 tablespoon soy sauce
440 g canned unsweetened crushed
    pineapple, reserve juice
2 teaspoons cornflour blended with
1 tablespoon water
2 shallots, cut in 2 cm lengths

Heat oil in a wok. Add garlic, pork and onion. Stir-fry 5 minutes. Add salt, soy sauce, pineapple and reserved juice.

Simmer covered 10 minutes. Bring to the boil and stir in blended cornflour and water to thicken. Add shallots and serve.

Serves 4

SWEET AND SOUR PORK

500 g lean pork, cut in 2 cm dice
½ teaspoon salt
1 tablespoon flour
1 teaspoon dry sherry
1 egg yolk
6 tablespoons cornflour
1 tablespoon vegetable oil
1 teaspoon chopped fresh ginger root
1 teaspoon chopped garlic
½ red capsicum, cut in 2 cm dice
½ green capsicum, cut in 2 cm dice
180 g Chinese mixed pickles, sliced
½ cup water (125 mL)
1 tablespoon cornflour
3 tablespoons sugar
3 tablespoons white vinegar
3 tablespoons tomato sauce
¼ cup pickle juice (60 mL)
1 ½ cups oil (375 mL), for deep-
    frying

Combine pork, salt, flour, sherry and egg yolk in a bowl. Let stand 15 minutes. Roll pork in cornflour just before deep-frying.

Heat oil in a saucepan. Add ginger and garlic, and stir-fry 30 seconds. Add capsicums and pickles. Blend water, cornflour, sugar, vinegar, tomato sauce and pickle juice. Stir into vegetables until mixture thickens. Keep warm.

Heat deep-frying oil. Cook pork in four batches for 5 minutes each. Remove and drain.

Reheat oil, refry pork 3–5 minutes. Drain well. Arrange on a serving platter. Spoon over sauce and serve at once.

Serves 6

Braised Pork Fillet in Peking Sauce (above) and Sweet and Sour Pork (below)

PORK SPARE RIBS WITH RED BEAN CURD

2 tablespoons oil
1 teaspoon chopped fresh ginger root
1 teaspoon chopped garlic
1 kg lean pork spare ribs, cut in 2.5 cm
   lengths
1 tablespoon soy sauce
1 tablespoon dry sherry or white wine
2 tablespoons red bean curd, mashed
2 cups pork stock (500 mL)
1 tablespoon cornflour (optional)

Heat oil in a wok. Add ginger, garlic and
pork spare ribs. Stir-fry over high heat
until brown. Pour off oil. Add soy sauce,
sherry, bean curd and stock. Bring to the
boil. Simmer covered until tender.
Thicken slightly with cornflour if necessary.

Serves 6-8

CHAR SUI (BARBECUED PORK)

750 g boneless pork
1 tablespoon honey combined with
1 tablespoon hot water

MARINADE

2 tablespoons soy sauce
1 ½ tablespoons dry sherry
3 tablespoons hoisin sauce
1 teaspoon five spice powder
1 teaspoon sesame paste
1 teaspoon brown sugar
1 slice fresh ginger root
1 clove garlic, crushed
2 tablespoons vegetable oil
dash red food colouring

Combine marinade ingredients in basin.
   Cut pork into strips 3 cm x 15 cm.
Pierce with a skewer. Add to marinade,
stirring to coat. Let stand 1 hour or overnight in refrigerator.
   Roast pork Chinese style on a rack
over a pan of water, at 200°C (400°F)
for 15 minutes. Baste with marinade.
Reduce heat to 175°C (340°F). Roast a
further 10 minutes.
   Brush pork with honey mixture on each
side, and continue cooking for 10 minutes.
   Slice pork thinly. Serve hot or cold or
in combination recipes.

Serves 4-6

Crisp Roast Belly of Pork
Rub salt into pricked pork skin.

Thoroughly coat meat with combined
sugar, soy and hoisin sauces and ginger.

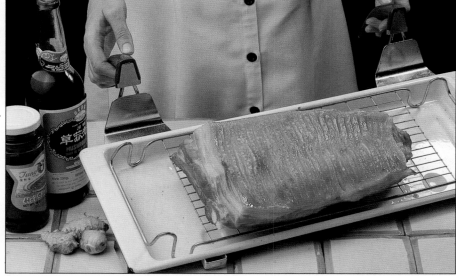
Roast 1 hour, until skin is crisp.

CRISP ROAST BELLY OF PORK

1 kg belly of pork
1 teaspoon salt
1 tablespoon brown sugar
3 tablespoons soy sauce
1 tablespoon hoisin sauce
½ teaspoon grated fresh ginger root
watercress (optional)
tomato roses (see Note) (optional)

Prick skin side of pork belly and rub salt
into skin. Mix sugar, soy and hoisin
sauces and ginger and rub into meat
side.
   Place meat, rind side up, on a rack
under a preheated griller and grill 15-20
minutes or until rind is crisp and brown.
Place meat, rind side up, on a rack over
a baking dish containing about 2 cm
water. Roast in a preheated oven at
180°C (350°F) for about 1 hour or until
cooked when tested. Let cool to room
temperature. Garnish with watercress
and tomato roses.

Note: Rind may be removed and served
separately. To prepare tomato roses, use
a small sharp knife and carefully peel tomatoes in a circular direction. Coil the strip
of tomato to resemble a rose. Secure
with a small pin if necessary.

Serves 6

BARBECUED SPARE RIBS

1 kg pork spare ribs
shallot curls
red and green chillies

BARBECUE SAUCE

2 cloves garlic, crushed
3 tablespoons soy sauce
1 tablespoon sherry
3 tablespoons hoisin sauce
1 tablespoon chicken stock
1 tablespoon oil

Combine sauce ingredients, pour over
ribs and marinate 3 hours, turning ribs
every hour.
   Place ribs on a rack over a baking dish
containing 2 cm water and roast in a
preheated oven at 200°C (400°F) until
cooked when tested. Garnish with shallot
curls and chillies.
   Serve on a bed of deep fried spring
rain noodles (vermicelli).

Note: Use belly pork cut into strips if
spareribs are not available.

Serves 4

Crisp Roast Belly of Pork

THE BEST OF BEEF

Chinese beef dishes come in many popular forms — Beef Chop Suey, Spicy Beef Satay, Party Beef Balls or Mongolian Hot Pot, for example. It pays to put in a little extra preparation time and marinate briefly; soy sauce, sherry and sliced ginger, for example, add a tangy touch to any meal.

SLICED BEEF WITH OYSTER SAUCE

1 ½ tablespoons vegetable oil
½ teaspoon chopped garlic
500 g grilling steak, thinly sliced (see Note)
1 teaspoon soy sauce
1 tablespoon dry sherry
¾ cup beef stock (185 mL)
1 tablespoon cornflour
2 tablespoons oyster sauce
1 teaspoon soy sauce
1 teaspoon sugar
½ teaspoon salt

Heat oil in a pan. Add garlic and stir briefly. Add a third of beef. Stir-fry 1 minute until it changes colour. Remove and repeat with remaining slices.

Return beef to pan. Add soy sauce and sherry, and cook for 1 minute. Pour in ½ cup stock (125 mL)

Blend cornflour with oyster sauce, remaining stock, soy sauce, sugar and salt. Stir in to thicken. Serve at once.

Note: To slice steak; cut into three or four portions. Place in freezer until firm. Cut thinly into diagonal slices.

Serves 6

SPICY BEEF SATAY

500 g grilling steak, cut in thin strips
1 tablespoon soy sauce
1 teaspoon sesame oil
2 teaspoons curry paste
3 tablespoons peanut butter or sesame paste
2 tablespoons dry sherry
2 tablespoons vegetable oil

Combine steak with soy sauce and sesame oil. Marinate 15 minutes. Soak bamboo satay sticks in water so they won't burn.

Thread three to four slices on each satay stick. Leave 2 cm at the pointed end of stick without meat. A thin strip of foil can be wound around the blunt end of each stick to decorate.

Combine curry paste, peanut butter and sherry. Spread thinly over beef. Brush with oil and cook under a preheated grill 1–2 minutes on each side.

Serves 4

CANTONESE BEEF

4 tablespoons vegetable oil
2 medium onions, finely shredded
4 large tomatoes, skinned, cut in eighths
1 teaspoon sugar
½ teaspoon salt
1 tablespoon black beans, chopped
1 teaspoon chopped fresh ginger root
1 teaspoon chopped garlic
500 g grilling steak, cut in thin strips
2 tablespoons soy sauce
1 cup beef stock (250 mL)
1 tablespoon cornflour blended with 2 tablespoons stock or water
shallot greens, sliced

Heat 2 tablespoons oil. Add onions, stir-fry 2 minutes. Add tomatoes, sugar and salt; stir-fry 1 minute. Cover and cook until tomatoes are just tender and retain shape. Remove to a bowl.

Heat remaining oil, add black beans, ginger and garlic. Stir-fry 1 minute. Add beef and cook over high heat until colour changes, 2-3 minutes. Add soy sauce, tomato mixture and beef stock.

Stir in blended cornflour and stock to thicken, without breaking tomato pieces. Serve garnished with shallot greens.

Serves 6

Spicy Beef Satay (left) and Cantonese Beef (right)

CURRIED BEEF

2–3 tablespoons vegetable oil
500 g onions, shredded
2 tablespoons chopped fresh ginger
 root
2 tablespoons curry powder or paste
500 g grilling steak, sliced
2 tablespoons sherry
1½ cups beef stock (375 mL)
2 teaspoons sugar
1 tablespoon canned coconut cream
2 tablespoons cornflour

Heat oil in a wok. Add onions and ginger, stir-fry 3 minutes. Add curry powder. Stir-fry to release flavours. Add beef, stir-fry over high heat until colour changes, 2–3 minutes.

Stir in sherry, 1 cup stock (250 mL), sugar and coconut cream. Simmer covered 3 minutes.

Blend cornflour with remaining stock. Stir in to thicken. Serve at once.

Serves 6

STEAMED BEEF BALLS WITH WATER CHESTNUTS

1 cup uncooked rice (200 g)
500 g topside steak, minced
3 shallots, finely chopped
1 teaspoon finely chopped fresh
 ginger root
2 water chestnuts, finely chopped
1 egg, lightly beaten
1 tablespoon soy sauce
2 teaspoons sherry
green vegetable leaves
soy sauce and chilli sauce, to serve

Place rice in a bowl, cover with water and soak for 1–1½ hours. Drain well and spread out on a tray to dry.

Combine steak, shallots, ginger, water chestnuts, egg, soy sauce and sherry; mix until well blended. Form mixture into balls about 4 cm in diameter.

Roll each ball in rice until completely covered. Place balls on green vegetables in a steamer basket, leaving enough space between so they don't touch each other.

Place in a steamer and steam for 30 minutes over gently boiling water. Serve with soy and chilli sauces for dipping.

Serves 4

Steamed Beef Balls
Prepare fresh ingredients by chopping finely.

Form mixture into balls and roll in rice to coat.

Place balls on green leafy vegetables in a steamer basket, leaving space between balls so they don't touch.

CELLOPHANE BEEF

170 g beef fillet
18 × 15 cm squares cellophane paper
1 tablespoon sesame oil
18 thin rings of carrot, parboiled
6 snow peas, stems removed, cut into thirds
1 medium onion, finely chopped
oil, for deep-frying
shredded lettuce, to serve

MARINADE

½ teaspoon chopped garlic
3 tablespoons soy sauce
1 tablespoon dry sherry
½ teaspoon sugar
¼ teaspoon pepper
1 tablespoon vegetable oil

Chill beef and cut into 18 thin slices.

Combine garlic, soy sauce, sherry, sugar, pepper and oil. Add beef and stir to coat. Marinate 1 hour. Discard marinade.

Arrange cellophane sheets in diamond shape. Brush each sheet lightly with sesame oil. Place one slice of carrot, snow pea and ½ teaspoon onion in centre of lower half of paper. Top with one slice of beef. Fold up lower corner to cover beef. Fold left and right corners to centre. Fold lower section up once more to centre line. Fold top corner down like an envelope and tuck in securely. Repeat until all the packages are made.

Heat oil to 150°C (300°F). Deep-fry a few envelopes at a time for 5 minutes. Drain well and arrange three envelopes each on six plates of shredded lettuce. Each diner breaks open the envelopes with chopsticks and eats the contents from the paper.

Serves 6

MINCING STEAK

For best results, buy topside steak and mince it yourself. There are two methods of mincing.

METHOD ONE

Trim the meat and cut into largish pieces. Use one or two cleavers, one in each hand, and keep chopping until the meat is minced. Place a damp kitchen cloth under the board to deaden the noise.

METHOD TWO

Trim the meat and mince in a processor or use a mincer.

BEEF CHOP SUEY

This famous name originated in San Francisco's China Town. It means 'mixture'.

3 tablespoons vegetable oil
½ teaspoon chopped garlic
½ teaspoon chopped fresh ginger root
1 shallot, cut in 2 cm lengths
250 g grilling steak, sliced thinly
125 g broccoli florets, blanched
125 g cauliflower florets, blanched
60 g champignons
60 g water chestnuts, sliced
60 g snow peas, stems removed
60 g bean sprouts, root removed
½ cup beef stock (125 mL)
1 tablespoon cornflour
1 tablespoon dry sherry
2 tablespoons soy sauce

Heat 1 ½ tablespoons oil. Add garlic, ginger and shallot, and stir-fry 1 minute. Add beef and stir-fry another minute. Remove from pan.

Heat remaining oil. Add broccoli, cauliflower, champignons, water chestnuts, snow peas and bean sprouts. Stir-fry 1–2 minutes. Add stock and return beef.

Blend cornflour with sherry and soy sauce. Stir in to thicken. Serve at once.

Serves 2–4

GINGERED BEEF

1 teaspoon grated fresh ginger root
⅓ cup soy sauce (80 mL)
2 teaspoons cornflour
500 g rump steak, trimmed and thinly sliced across the grain
4 Chinese mushrooms, soaked in warm water 20 minutes
¼ cup oil (60 mL)
5 cm piece fresh ginger root, shredded
125 g canned bamboo shoots, drained and diced

In a large bowl combine grated ginger, soy sauce and cornflour.

Add meat and mix well. Allow to marinate for 1 hour, stirring occasionally. Drain mushrooms, remove stems and discard. Slice mushroom caps.

Remove meat from marinade and reserve. Heat oil in a wok over moderate heat. Add ginger and stir-fry for 3 minutes. Add meat, bamboo shoots and mushrooms and stir-fry until meat is cooked. Add marinade and heat through. Serve on a bed of rice or boiled noodles.

Serves 4

Gingered Beef

MONGOLIAN HOT POT

500 g lamb or rump steak
2 onions, cut in wedges
1 bunch shallots, sliced
125 g snow peas
125 g Chinese cabbage, sliced
125 g bean sprouts
1 red capsicum, cut in wedges
125 g bean curd
125 g egg noodles, cooked
1 quantity meat stock

Remove fat from meat and slice thinly across the grain. Arrange meat, vegetables and noodles attractively on a large serving platter.

Heat an electric wok or casserole on a portable heating unit at the table. Bring stock to the boil. Using small wire baskets, guests select and cook their own food in boiling stock. At end of the meal, remaining vegetables, meat and noodles are added to stock and served as a soup.

Serves 4

STIR-FRIED BEEF AND CELERY

500 g rump steak, trimmed
½ bunch celery
2 tablespoons sherry
2 tablespoons soy sauce
½ teaspoon sesame oil
3 teaspoons cornflour
4 tablespoons oil
½ cup chicken stock (125 mL)
2 tablespoons water

Cut beef across the grain into thin strips. String celery if necessary, then slice diagonally.

Combine sherry, soy sauce, sesame oil and 2 teaspoons cornflour in a bowl. Add beef and toss to coat. Stand about 10 minutes.

Heat half the oil in a wok. Add beef and stir-fry, in two batches, for 3 minutes each. Remove beef and keep warm.

Heat remaining oil in the wok, add celery and stir-fry for 1 minute. Add chicken stock and simmer for 2–2½ minutes.

Return beef to wok and heat through. Blend remaining 1 teaspoon cornflour with water, add to wok and stir until thickened.

Serves 4

BEEF WITH SNOW PEAS

500 g snow peas
3 tablespoons oil
2 teaspoons oyster sauce
500 g rump steak
2 cloves garlic, finely chopped
2 thin slices fresh ginger root, shredded
1 tablespoon soy sauce
1 red chilli, seeded and sliced

Top and tail snow peas and wipe with a damp cloth if necessary. Heat 1 tablespoon oil in a wok, add snow peas and stir-fry for 1 minute. Add oyster sauce and toss to coat. Remove and keep warm.

Trim meat and cut into four pieces. Heat remaining oil, add meat, garlic and ginger and cook until meat is sealed on both sides. Remove and cut meat into strips. Return to the wok and continue stir-frying for a further 5 minutes. Sprinkle with soy sauce. Serve topped with sliced chilli.

Note: If snow peas are not in season, Chinese broccoli or spinach may be substituted.

Serves 4

PARTY BEEF BALLS

1 kg lean beef, minced twice
2 eggs, beaten
4 tablespoons plain flour
½ teaspoon salt
pinch pepper
1 ½ cups oil (375 mL) for deep-frying

SAUCE

2 tablespoons vegetable oil
1 teaspoon chopped garlic
1 tablespoon red capsicum, cut in
    1 cm dice
1 tablespoon green capsicum, cut in
    1 cm dice
1 tablespoon bamboo shoots, cut in
    1 cm dice
1 tablespoon pineapple, cut in
    1 cm dice
1 cup sugar (250 g)
1 cup white vinegar (250 mL)
1 cup water (250 mL)
2 tablespoons soy sauce
2 tablespoons tomato sauce
3 tablespoons cornflour blended with
    ½ cup water (125 mL)

Shape mince with wet hands into balls 2 cm in diameter. Combine egg, flour, salt and pepper to form a batter. Pour over beef balls to coat.

Heat oil for deep-frying. Add about six balls at a time, fry until golden; drain.

Arrange on a serving platter or thread on satay sticks.

To make sauce, heat oil in a wok. Add garlic, vegetables and pineapple, stir-fry 3 minutes. Stir in sugar, vinegar, water, soy and tomato sauces. Stir in blended cornflour to thicken.

Spoon sauce over balls or serve separately in a bowl.

Serves 8–10

RED SIMMERED BEEF

1 kg piece topside steak
3 tablespoons oil
1 clove garlic, crushed
2 thin slices fresh ginger root, finely
    chopped
½ cup soy sauce (125 ml)
⅓ cup sherry (80 mL)
water, to cover
2 whole star anise
1 small piece cinnamon stick

Tie meat at 5 cm intervals so that it will hold its shape while cooking. Heat oil in a wok. Brown beef on all sides over high heat. Add remaining ingredients.

Bring liquid to a boil over high heat. Reduce heat, cover the wok and simmer for 1½ hours, turning beef every 30 minutes.

Slice beef and serve hot or cold with some of the sauce.

Note: The sauce can be refrigerated and kept for use in other dishes. If the sauce is heated to boiling point every few days, it will keep for several weeks.

Serves 6

Red Simmered Beef
Brown beef on all sides in hot oil.

Slice beef and serve hot or cold with
some of the cooking sauce.

FILLET STEAK CHINESE-STYLE

375 g piece fillet steak
1 tablespoon soy sauce
1 tablespoon hoisin sauce
1 tablespoon dry sherry
pinch five spice powder
2 tablespoons oil
¼ teaspoon salt
1 large onion, peeled and cut into eighths
½ teaspoon chopped fresh ginger root
1 teaspoon chopped garlic
1 level tablespoon cornflour
3 tablespoons beef stock
½ teaspoon sesame oil
shallot greens, to serve

Freeze beef briefly until firm, then cut into thin slices. Combine beef, soy and hoisin sauces, sherry and five spice, and marinate for 15 minutes. Remove beef and set marinade aside.

Heat 1 tablespoon oil in a pan. Add salt and onion and stir-fry 1 minute. Remove onion with a slotted spoon and set aside. Reheat remaining tablespoon of oil in pan and add ginger, garlic and beef. Stir-fry 1–2 minutes, until beef just loses its pinkness. Do not overcook or it willl become tough. Return onion to pan.

Blend cornflour and stock and stir in to thicken. Sprinkle over sesame oil and serve garnished with shallot greens. This recipe can also be served on a sizzle plate.

Serves 6

Fillet Steak Chinese-style

COOKING CLASS

Chinese cooking is easy when you know how. In the following pages, we look at cooking utensils and how to use them, and the basic methods of cooking Chinese-style. The rest is a little practice, a little experimenting, and lots of visits to your local Chinese restaurant to compare results.

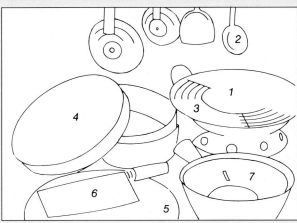

1 Wok
2 Charn (stirring ladle)
3 Strainer
4 Steamer
5 Chopping board
6 Cleaver
7 Clay pot

BASIC KITCHEN UTENSILS

We all have our own favourite knives, pots and pans for cooking, and these can be used with great success for Chinese cooking. In a Chinese kitchen, the utensils are very few but practical, namely the wok, wok charn, cleavers, strainers and chopsticks.

The wok is a thin metal all purpose cooking pan, with high sides and rounded bottom. It can be used for stir-frying, deep-frying, parboiling. simmering, braising, boiling and steaming. By placing a set of steaming baskets into the wok, a first class steamer is made, which will enable as many as five different dishes to be cooked at the one time. e.g. fish, dim sum, egg rolls, chicken or duck, rice and sponges. The wok is also ideal for making omelettes and for outdoor cooking.

The wok charn is designed to fit the curvature of the wok. It is used mainly for stir-fry dishes, to turn food and prevent burning, or sticking.

Light and heavy cleavers are both made from tempered steel; the light cleaver is used for slicing meat and vegetables and the heavy is used for chopping through bones, crab and lobster shells. The reverse edge is used for mashing and when held upright, the handle serves as a grinder for spices and black beans.

The flat edges are used for transferring chopped food from the board to serving plates, pounding and tenderising meats, crushing ginger and garlic and, when combined with the light cleaver, forms an excellent mincer.

Strainers are used for removing deep-fried foods from hot oil, draining off excess oil and in the making of potato and noodle baskets.

Chopsticks come in various sizes, with an extra long size to be used in the kitchen suitable for beating eggs, adding and removing food from a deep-fryer, turning food while cooking, adding beaten egg to soups, forming egg flower patterns, and removing ingredients from jars.

Optional extras include *steam boats* for Mongolian hot pot, *small cooking baskets* for steam boat cookery and a *tong hock* for measuring and transferring liquids.

1 Dried mushrooms
2 White radish
3 Garlic
4 Fresh ginger root
5 Shallots
6 Bean sprouts
7 Snow peas
8 Baby or mini corn
9 Fresh coriander
10 Chillies
11 Lotus Root
12 Capsicum
13 Tangerine

Stir-frying: prepare vegetables in advance.

Heat oil in a wok until very hot. Fry garlic and ginger first to flavour oil.

Add larger, denser vegetables and pour in sauce or stock.

CHINESE METHODS OF COOKING

The main styles of cooking are: stir-frying, steaming, deep-frying and roasting, all with a minimum of fuel, which in former days was a matter of necessity. In early days wood, coal and charcoal were used. Today all these forms of cooking are carried out with modern gas and electric ranges, electric woks and microwave ovens, still with consideration towards economy.

Stir-frying

This technique is used for tender cuts of pork and beef, poultry, seafood and vegetables. The ingredients are sliced, shredded, diced or minced, then stir-fried in a wok using a wok charn. Cook over high heat in the minimum of oil. This method seals in the natural juices and preserves colour, texture and flavour.

Gas is preferred for Chinese cooking for the instant control of temperature. If using an electric stove, flat-bottomed woks are available from most Chinese foodstores.

Ingredients are added to the wok in order of texture and cooking time. The preparation of ingredients and being well organised, is the key to success for Chinese cooking:

- Collect all ingredients required for the recipe. Allow time for soaking dried ingredients like Chinese mushrooms.
- Slice meat, poultry and seafood. Arrange in order of cooking on a kitchen tray. Prepare marinades if required, and marinate. This can take up to 30 minutes.

- Wash, drain and cut vegetables to size. Parboil or blanch if necessary.
- Measure liquid ingredients like oil, sauces, stock and seasonings. Blend any thickening agent with stock or water and stir before adding to wok. Chop ginger, garlic and chillies. Arrange ingredients in the order that they will be added to the wok for cooking.
- Collect cooking utensils and warm serving dishes.

This basic preparation should be done for all recipes before any style of Chinese cooking is started as it makes Chinese cooking easy. Confucius once said, "Cooked Chinese food waits not for any man". It should be served and eaten at once, to experience the best flavour, texture and colour of the food.

Deep-frying

The deep-frying technique is used extensively throughout Chinese cuisine, from hors d'oeuvres to main course dishes and desserts. You can use a great variety of ingredients, such as pork, beef, poultry, seafood, vegetables, various types of noodles, skins for wrapping as well as fruit.

Deep-frying ingredients are cut into even-sized pieces and dipped into a protective coating of batter, such as seasoned flour, beaten egg and breadcrumbs, spring roll or wonton skins, even cellophane paper can be used to protect ingredients. Then they are immersed in hot oil to cover, until cooked.

Oil or lard should be heated to 180°C (350°F) in a deep-fryer or deep-sided saucepan, not more than half full. If a saucepan is used without a thermometer, a slice of fresh ginger root can be added to indicate the oil's temperature. When the ginger is golden, the oil is the correct temperature for deep-frying.

On reaching 180°C (350°F) oil or lard will cease to bubble, and a faint blue haze will start to rise.

Tips

— Ingredients can be marinated then drained before dipping into batter and being fried.
— Ingredients can be two-thirds cooked, then drained. Just prior to serving, oil can be reheated to the correct temperature, and the final stage of deep-frying completed. This gives even cooking and a crisp texture. This method is called double-frying.
— Only add small quantities of ingredients to the oil at one time. This maintains the oil's temperature and prevents absorption.
— When cooking is completed, drain food thoroughly and serve with prepared dips or sauces.
— Allow oil to cool then strain. Store covered to prevent dust from settling on the surface. Add a quantity of fresh oil to pre-used oil before re-using, this prevents oil from discolouring and gives a higher smoke point when reheating.

Roasting

Roasting in China originally took place outdoors on large spits or used hanging hooks over open fires. Over

Even large ingredients, such as chicken, can be deep-fried in a wok, providing you blanch them in boiling water first

When cooked, leave deep-fried foods on a rack to cool and drain off excess oil

Prepare fresh ingredients by chopping finely

hundreds of years, the Chinese people have bought roast duck and chicken, cuts of roast and barbecued pork, from their local roast meat shops, which also supply fresh pork, duck and chicken. Due to the fact that households did not have refrigerators or stoves for roasting, small portions of cooked meats were purchased as required before meals were prepared.

The Chinese style of roasting can be done in the modern stove by making wire hooks and hanging, from the top shelf of the oven, marinated duck, chicken or strips of pork brushed with barbecue sauce, with a roasting dish containing several centimetres of water placed underneath to catch the drips.

Roasting can also be done by placing a cake rack over a roasting pan containing 2–5 cm of water, and placing the meats onto the rack. Meat should not sit flat in a roasting dish stewing in its own juices as it tends to become tough.

Roasting starts on a high heat and is later reduced to medium. It is usual to baste during cooking with marinades or honey blended with warm water.

Steaming

Cooking by the steaming method enables three to five preparations to be cooked at the one time, over the minimum of fuel. Chinese steaming baskets are made from bamboo and consist of two baskets and a lid. They come in various sizes, and extra baskets can be purchased individually. A new bamboo steamer should be soaked in water overnight, before using the first time. Chinese metal steamers are also available. They have two baskets with a lid and a boiler-style base, and can be used for direct and indirect steaming. The base and lid can serve as a boiler, or be used for stewing long-cooking ingredients.

Direct steaming

Bamboo steamers are placed into a wok containing several centimetres of vigorously boiling water. Food to be steamed can be placed on a heatproof plate or tray, or on banana leaves cut to basket size, Chinese cabbage or lettuce leaves. Always leave enough room for the steam to circulate around the food and cook it by direct contact. Place a clean cloth over the top basket before putting the lid on. This will absorb condensation and prevent it from dripping onto the steamed products.

Many varieties of yum cha dumplings with various fillings, dim sum, gow gees, savoury custards, pork and fish balls and spare ribs are steamed; as well as whole fish and poultry, beef and pork dishes, vegetables, cakes and puddings.

Steaming time varies with different foods. Dumplings and dim sum take 20 minutes, a whole fish weighing 750 g will cook in 15 minutes, sponges and cakes cook in 30 minutes, while medium-sized chickens and larger cuts of pork take 40 minutes. The longer cooking items are placed in the lower baskets and other baskets are placed on top in order of cooking times.

Indirect steaming

This is usually done in a heatproof basin, which can be covered with aluminium foil. The basin is placed in a large saucepan or boiler with its ingredients. Boiling water is added to surround the basin to about half its height. Then the saucepan lid is added. The water must remain boiling during the cooking time. Check water level when steaming. Extra boiling water should be added if necessary for both methods of steaming.

Food cooked by indirect steaming includes: whole ducks, whole chickens, slow-cooked stewed meats and savoury custards. It is also an effective method for reheating rice. Steamed food is best slightly undercooked, as it continues cooking in its own stored heat after being removed from the steamer.

Simmer cooking

This gentle method of cooking is used for soups and long cooking of less tender cuts of meat. It is also suitable for seafoods to avoid over cooking. A stock or sauce is brought to the boil with the ingredients added, then simmered over a low heat until tender.

Parboiling

Parboiling is used when cooking ingredients of different textures. The tougher varieties are added to boiling stock or water for a short time to commence the cooking process. They are then refreshed in iced water to set colour and prevent overcooking in stored heat. The cooking time, when tender ingredients are added, will then be the same.

Chinese fire pot cooking

The Chinese fire pot is a good example of simmer cooking. It enables a larger number of diners to be catered for and to participate in the cooking which is done at the table.

Fire pots or steam boats as they are also called are available from Chinese foodstores. They are made from a variety of metals which include brass. Individual wire baskets or chopsticks are used to cook the food in small quantities, in simmering stock. Hot coals or heat beads are placed into the chimney in the centre of the cooking container. This keeps the stock simmering. An electric frying pan can substitute for the fire pot.

The fire pot is placed in the centre of the dining table on a heatproof tray or on a cutting board covered with aluminium foil. Boiling stock is poured into the container, and the raw ingredients and condiments are placed around the pot.

Each diner selects and cooks food which is dipped into various sauces or raw egg. Steamed rice and Chinese tea are served with the meal, which can last several hours.

A fire pot or steam boat is used to cook dishes such as Mongolian Hot Pot

SAUCY CHICKEN FAVOURITES

Choose the freshest poultry available from a reputable supplier, and dress up your chicken with delicious sauces, to serve family favourites like Braised Chicken and Almonds, Shanghai-style Chicken and Honey Lemon Chicken.

Trays: The Australian East India Company Pty Ltd

SHANGHAI-STYLE CHICKEN

1 medium onion, chopped
1 carrot, chopped
1 stalk celery, chopped
6 fresh parsley stalks
1 slice fresh ginger root
1 teaspoon white peppercorns
2 bay leaves
1.5 litres cold water
1.5 kg chicken
2 bunches fresh green asparagus
2 tablespoons toasted sesame seeds,
    to sprinkle

SAUCE

2 tablespoons vegetable oil
1 onion, finely sliced
½ teaspoon chopped garlic
2 red chillies, seeded and chopped
1 tablespoon oyster sauce
1 tablespoon soy sauce
1 cup chicken stock (250 mL)
salt and pepper
1 tablespoon cornflour

Cook chicken by placing vegetables, seasonings and water into a large saucepan. Bring to the boil, add chicken and simmer until tender. Remove chicken meat from carcass in strips. Set aside.

Cut 1–2 cm from root end of each asparagus stalk if tough. Scrape stems lightly with a peeler or small sharp knife. Wash well.

Re-tie asparagus in bunches. Cook in boiling salted water 6–8 minutes. Refresh in cold water.

To make sauce, heat oil in a saucepan. Saute onion and garlic 2–3 minutes and add chillies. Blend oyster sauce, soy sauce, stock, salt, pepper and cornflour together. Add to onion mixture and stir until boiling.

Arrange cooked asparagus on a serving platter. Top with chicken strips. Spoon sauce over chicken and sprinkle with sesame seeds. Serve hot.

Quick Variation
Use canned asparagus spears. Cook chicken in a microwave on HIGH for 27 minutes. Prepare sauce while chicken is cooking.

Serves 6–8

FIVE SPICE CHICKEN

1.5 kg chicken
4 shallots, shredded

MARINADE

1 teaspoon chopped garlic
3 tablespoons soy sauce
2 tablespoons vegetable oil
½ teaspoon five spice powder
½ teaspoon sugar

Combine marinade ingredients. Brush mixture inside and over chicken. Let stand 30 minutes on a rack over a pan of water.

Drain chicken and roast Chinese style at 180°C (350°F) until tender. Baste and turn chicken four times during cooking for even browning.

Chop chicken Chinese style (see Preparation Techniques). Serve hot garnished with shallot shreds.

Quick Variation
Place drained chicken in a glass dish on a microwave roasting rack.

Cook uncovered 27 minutes on HIGH, turning and basting every 10 minutes.

Serves 6–8

Five Spice Chicken (left) and Shanghai-style Chicken (right)

CRISP SPICED CHICKEN

1.5 kg chicken
1 teaspoon five spice powder
1 tablespoon cornflour
oil, for deep-frying
lemon wedges and
    shallot curls to garnish

Wash and clean chicken. Dry thoroughly and chop through the bone into 10 or 12 pieces (see Preparation Techniques). Combine five spice powder and cornflour and toss with chicken.

Heat oil in a wok and deep-fry chicken pieces in batches, for 5 minutes; drain well. Reheat the oil and deep-fry chicken until golden brown and cooked. Drain on absorbent kitchen paper.

Garnish with lemon wedges and shallots. Serve hot with Chinese Rice (see recipe).

Note: If you find five spice powder very pungent, reduce the quantity to ½ teaspoon the first time you make the dish.

Serves 4

CHICKEN WITH WALNUTS

1 tablespoon cornflour
1 egg white, lightly beaten
500 g chicken breast, skinned, boned
    and cut in strips
1 cup oil (250 mL)
250 g walnut halves
1 teaspoon sugar
1 tablespoon soy sauce
2 tablespoons dry sherry
fresh coriander leaves and sliced red
    chilli, to garnish

Mix cornflour and egg white. Add chicken and coat evenly on all sides.

Heat oil in a wok. Deep-fry chicken, in batches, for 2 minutes; drain well. Reheat the oil and deep-fry chicken until golden. Drain and keep warm on a serving dish. Pour off all but 1 tablespoon oil from wok. Add walnuts, reduce heat and stir-fry 1 minute. Remove and sprinkle nuts over chicken.

Add sugar, soy sauce and sherry to wok and simmer 2 minutes. Remove from heat and pour over chicken or serve separately.

Garnish with coriander leaves and sliced red chilli.

Note: Walnuts are often bitter when fried. To remove the bitterness, peel them by simmering for 1 minute then drain and remove the skin with a skewer. Dry thoroughly.

Serves 4

Crisp Spiced Chicken

CHILLI CHICKEN AND CASHEWS

500 g boned chicken, cut in 2 cm dice
2 teaspoons cornflour
1 tablespoon soy sauce
1 tablespoon dry sherry
2 tablespoons chicken stock
2 teaspoons cornflour
1 tablespoon brown sugar
1 tablespoon vinegar
1 tablespoon soy sauce
1½ cups oil, for deep frying (375 mL)
1 teaspoon Szechuan peppercorns
4–6 dried chillies, halved if large
1 teaspoon chopped fresh ginger root
2 shallots, cut in 3 cm lengths
½ teaspoon sesame oil
½ cup toasted cashews (160 g)

Combine diced chicken, cornflour, soy sauce and sherry. Marinate 15 minutes. Blend stock, cornflour, sugar, vinegar and soy sauce and set aside.

Heat oil and deep-fry chicken until white. Remove and drain on absorbent kitchen paper.

Heat 2 tablespoons oil with Szechuan peppercorns. When oil is hot, remove peppercorns (this gives the oil an aromatic flavour). Add chillies to oil and fry until black. Stir in ginger and shallots. Add stock mixture and stir to thicken sauce. Return chicken, stir-fry 3 minutes. Sprinkle with sesame oil. Fold in cashew nuts. Serve hot.

Serves 6

SILVER THREAD SALAD

500 g chicken breast
oil, for deep frying
60 g vermicelli, cut in 5 cm lengths
250 g bean sprouts, root removed

DRESSING

½ teaspoon salt
2 teaspoons sugar
2 teaspoons white vinegar
2 teaspoons ginger wine
¼ teaspoon chilli oil or sauce
1 tablespoon sesame soy or sesame
    oil

Cover chicken breast with cold water in a pan. Bring to the boil. Remove from heat and let stand 8 minutes. Repeat cooking and standing time once more. Drain chicken, reserving liquid. Remove skin and bones and shred chicken meat into fine strips.

Heat oil. Add vermicelli in small amounts which will puff up instantly. Turn with tongs and avoid colouring. Remove and drain. Lightly crush vermicelli with hands. This step can be done in advance.

Blanch bean sprouts in boiling chicken liquid. Refresh in cold water and drain.

Combine chicken, vermicelli and bean sprouts on a serving platter. Set aside to chill.

Combine dressing ingredients. Pour over salad and toss just before serving.

Serves 6

RED ROAST CHICKEN

4 tablespoons hoisin sauce
pinch Chinese red food colouring
2 tablespoons dry sherry or water
1.5 kg chicken

Combine hoisin sauce, red food colouring and sherry. Brush over chicken and let stand several hours; drain chicken.

Roast Chinese style on a rack over a pan of water at 180°C (350°F) for 1½ hours or until tender. Turn and baste chicken every 20 minutes.

Chop into serving pieces and serve hot or cold.

Quick Variation
Place drained chicken in a glass dish on microwave roasting rack. Cook uncovered for 27 minutes on HIGH, turning and basting every 10 minutes.

Serves 6–8

BRAISED CHICKEN AND ALMONDS

500 g boned chicken, cut in 2 cm dice
1 tablespoon soy sauce
½ teaspoon salt
1 tablespoon dry sherry
125 g carrot, cut in 2 cm dice
125 g beans, cut in 2 cm dice
1 cup oil, for deep-frying (250 mL)
4 tablespoons vegetable oil
½ teaspoon chopped fresh ginger root
½ teaspoon chopped garlic
1 onion, cut in 2 cm dice
1 stalk celery cut in 2 cm dice
4 Chinese mushrooms, soaked in
    warm water 20 minutes and cut in
    2 cm dices
125 g bamboo shoot, cut in 2 cm dice
¾ cup chicken stock (180 mL)
1½ tablespoons oyster sauce
3 teaspoons cornflour blended with
    1 tablespoon water
2 shallots, cut in 2 cm dice
125 g almonds, toasted

Combine chicken pieces, soy sauce, salt and sherry. Parboil carrots and beans until crispy tender. Rinse in cold water.

Heat oil for deep-frying and add chicken cubes in small quantities. When white, remove and drain.

Heat 2 tablespoons oil, add ginger, garlic and vegetables in order of texture; onion, celery, beans, carrot, mushrooms and bamboo shoot. Stir-fry over high heat. Add stock and cook covered 2 minutes. Remove from pan.

Heat 2 tablespoons of oil, add chicken and stir-fry over high heat 3 minutes. Return vegetables and stir in oyster sauce. Add blended cornflour and water. Fold in shallots and half of the almonds.

Serve garnished with remaining almonds.

Serves 6–8

PREPARATION TECHNIQUES

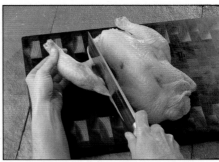

To section a chicken: remove leg and thigh by cutting lengthways between thigh and breast.

Halve chicken by cutting along the backbone from the parson's nose to the neck.

Remove wings and separate drumsticks from thighs at the joint.

Divide wings into two pieces at the joints, and chop drumsticks and thighs into three pieces each. Slice breasts into three or four pieces depending on size of chicken.

HONEY LEMON CHICKEN

1 kg fresh chicken pieces (e.g. thighs, drumsticks)
2 tablespoons soy sauce
1 tablespoon dry sherry
juice 2 lemons, strained
2–3 tablespoons honey
2 tablespoons vegetable oil
1 teaspoon chopped fresh ginger root
1 teaspoon chopped garlic
1/4 teaspoon salt
1 1/2 cups chicken stock or water (375 mL)
1 tablespoon cornflour blended with 2 tablespoons cold water
slices of fresh lemon to garnish

Pierce chicken pieces with a skewer. Combine soy sauce, sherry, lemon juice and honey. Brush over chicken pieces and let stand 30 minutes.

Heat oil. Add ginger, garlic and salt. Add drained chicken pieces and brown evenly. Pour off excess oil, add marinade and stock. Simmer covered 45 minutes until tender. Turn chicken pieces twice during cooking. Remove chicken and place on a serving platter. Stir blended cornflour and water into sauce. When boiling, strain and spoon over chicken pieces. Serve garnished with lemon.

Serves 6

BRAISED CHICKEN WITH PEKING SAUCE

500 g boned chicken breast, sliced
1/2 teaspoon salt
1 egg white, beaten
1 1/2 cups vegetable oil (375 mL)
1 clove garlic, crushed
1 slice fresh ginger root
1 tablespoon vegetable oil
2 onions, cut in eighths
1 red capsicum, cut in 2 cm dice
2 tablespoons hoisin sauce
1 tablespoon dry sherry
60 g vermicelli noodles

Mix chicken slices with salt and egg white.

Heat oil. Add garlic and ginger, remove when brown. Fry chicken pieces until white. Drain well on kitchen paper.

Heat 1 tablespoon oil. Add onions and capsicum, stir-fry 2 minutes. Stir in hoisin sauce, sherry and chicken to reheat.

Cut noodles into 5 cm lengths. Fry in hot oil until they puff up. Drain well on kitchen paper. Arrange on a serving platter and top with onion mixture.

Serves 6

Smoked Chicken (left),
and Braised Chicken (right)
and Peking Sauce

SMOKED CHICKEN

1.5 kg chicken
2 tablespoons brown peppercorns
1 tablespoon salt
2 litres water
4 shallots
3 slices fresh ginger root
2 whole star anise
1 cinnamon stick
1 cup soy sauce (250 mL)
½ cup sugar (125 g)
½ cup plain flour (60 g)
½ cup dry tea leaves (60 g)
1 tablespoon sesame oil

Clean and wipe chicken. Fry peppercorns and salt for 1 minute in a wok. Rub into chicken and allow to stand for 2 hours.

Bring water to the boil in a large pan. Add shallots, ginger, star anise, cinnamon and soy sauce and simmer 10 minutes. Add chicken and cook for 10 minutes over low heat, turning once. Remove chicken and allow to cool.

Put sugar, flour and tea leaves in a wok, and cover with a rack. Sit chicken on its side on rack. Cover tightly and smoke for 45 minutes to 1 hour, over a low heat, turning chicken halfway through. Remove chicken from wok and brush with sesame oil; cool.

Chop Chinese style (see Preparation Techniques) and arrange on a platter.

Serves 6

WHITE COOKED CHICKEN

1.5 kg chicken
½ bunch shallots, sliced
3 slices fresh ginger root
Sherry-Soy Dip (see recipe)

Truss chicken and place it whole into a large wok with enough boiling water to cover. Add shallots and ginger. Bring to the boil, reduce heat, cover and cook chicken for 12 minutes. Turn chicken, cover and simmer another 10 minutes.

Remove wok from heat and allow chicken to cool in the liquid. Cut chicken legs and wings into 5 cm sections, cutting through the bone with a heavy cleaver. Arrange slices of breast meat in the centre of a serving plate. Place sections of wing, leg and thigh around the breast. Serve cold with Sherry-Soy Dip.

Serves 6

Sweet and Sour Sesame Chicken

SWEET AND SOUR SESAME CHICKEN

1.5 kg chicken, jointed
3 tablespoons plum sauce
1 tablespoon vinegar
2 cups chicken stock (500 mL)
⅓ cup dry sherry (80 mL)
1 tablespoon finely chopped fresh
   ginger root
1 onion, quartered
160 g canned straw mushrooms
2 stalks celery, sliced
220 g canned water chestnuts
220 g canned bamboo shoots, drained
   and sliced
2 tablespoons cornflour blended with
   water
1 tablespoon sesame seeds

Preheat oven to 180°C (350°F).

Arrange chicken in an ovenproof dish. Combine plum sauce, vinegar, stock, sherry and ginger and pour over chicken. Cover and bake 40 minutes.

Add vegetables, return to oven and cook a further 15 minutes. Remove chicken and vegetables to a heated serving dish.

Thicken remaining liquid with blended cornflour and water. Bring to the boil and simmer 2 minutes. Pour over chicken. Sprinkle with sesame seeds and serve hot with Chinese Rice (see recipe).

Serves 6

BRAISED CHICKEN AND VEGETABLES

3 tablespoons oil
1 teaspoon chopped garlic
1 teaspoon chopped fresh ginger root
500 g boned chicken breast,
    shredded
1 tablespoon soy sauce
2 tablespoons dry sherry
½ teaspoon sugar
¼ teaspoon salt
1 onion, cut in eighths
300 g broccoli, broken into florets
100 g mushrooms, sliced
1 cup chicken stock (250 mL)
2 teaspoons cornflour blended with
2 tablespoons water

Heat half the oil in a wok. Add garlic, ginger and shredded chicken. Stir-fry over high heat for 3 minutes. Add soy sauce, sherry, sugar and salt. Simmer covered 1 minute. Remove from wok and set aside.

Heat remaining oil. Add onion, broccoli and mushrooms. Stir fry 2 minutes. Add chicken and stock. Cook covered 2 minutes.

Stir blended cornflour and water into mixture until boiling.

Serves 6

BRAISED CHICKEN AND BLACK BEAN SAUCE

2 tablespoons vegetable oil
½ teaspoon chopped garlic
2 teaspoons black beans, chopped
500 g boned chicken, cut in 2 cm dice
1 tablespoon sherry
½ teaspoon sugar
2 teaspoons soy sauce
pinch pepper
3 tablespoons chicken stock
2 tomatoes, peeled, and cut in 2 cm
    dice
3 teaspoons cornflour blended with
    3 tablespoons water
4 shallot flowers, for garnish

Heat oil in a wok. Add garlic and beans and stir-fry 1 minute. Add chicken and cook over high heat 3 minutes. Add sherry, sugar, soy sauce, pepper and stock. Cook covered 3 minutes. Stir in tomatoes and blended cornflour water. Cook until boiling and thickened.

Serves 6

TANGY DUCK DELIGHTS

Some of the most famous Chinese dishes have been created around the distinctive flavour of duck. Classics like Peking Duck, Roast Duck with Plum Sauce, and Eight Jewel Duck are perfect for entertaining.

PEKING DOILIES

1 ¼ cups water (310 mL)
2 cups sifted flour (250 g)
oil or sesame oil, or a combination of
    the two

In a pan, bring water to the boil. Add flour, all at once, and stir very quickly with a wooden spoon to combine. Remove from pan and knead mixture on a floured board until smooth, about 10 minutes. Cover with a damp towel and stand for 10 minutes.

Form the dough into a long roll 3 cm in diameter. Cut into 1 cm thick slices. Flatten to a 6 mm thickness and brush one side of half the rounds with a little oil. Place one unoiled round on top of the oiled side of another. Dust each pair with flour and roll out to a very thin pancake, about 10–12 cm in diameter. Roll from the centre, turning the pancake a little after each roll to ensure a perfect circle of even thickness.

Heat an ungreased wok or griddle over low to medium heat. Bake one pancake at a time for about 1 minute on each side or until lightly coloured.

Transfer to a platter, separate the two halves and keep covered with a towel until all pancakes are ready. Peking doilies can be made in advance, kept in the refrigerator and reheated by steaming for 8–10 minutes.

Makes 15–25 doilies (depending on thickness)

PEKING DUCK

2 kg duck
½–¾ cup water (125–180 mL)
4 tablespoons honey
Peking doilies (see recipe)
shallot curls
½ cucumber
½–¾ cup hoisin sauce or plum
    sauce (125–180 mL)

Choose a fresh duck with neck and skin intact. Wash duck, immerse in boiling water, lift out and dry thoroughly inside and out. Hang duck overnight in a cool airy place, to allow the skin to dry thoroughly.

Dissolve honey in water and brush skin until completely saturated with honey. Hang duck to dry completely for about 6 hours or until the skin is dry and slightly hardened by the honey.

Meanwhile, prepare Peking doilies and shallot curls. Peel cucumber and cut in half lengthways. Scoop out the seedy centre part and cut into strips.

To separate the skin from the flesh of the duck, insert a straw immediately underneath the skin and blow through it. Place duck on a rack over a drip pan. Roast in a 180°C (350°F) oven without basting for 1½–2 hours or until skin is browned and crisp.

With a very sharp knife, slice off skin and cut into squares. Carve meat in thick slices and serve separately during the meal. Take a doily and top with one or two pieces of skin, shallot curls, cucumber strips and hoisin sauce. Roll doily to eat.

Note: Sometimes only the skin is eaten and the meat used as an ingredient for other dishes.

Serves 6

Peking Duck served with Peking Doilies

Plate and bowl: Royal Doulton Australia Pty Ltd

CRISPY CRUNCHY VEGETABLES

Chinese vegetables make superb accompaniments, designed to enhance rather than compete with the other flavours and textures of a meal. Vegetables should never be overcooked — cook very briefly, leaving the texture slightly crunchy. Dishes like Stir-fried Sweet and Sour Vegetables or Asparagus in the Snow, go well with steamed rice; other dishes, like Vermicelli and Vegetables, can make a meal on their own.

STEAMED BITTER MELONS

4 medium bitter melons

FILLING

250 g soft bean curd or canned gluten, finely chopped
1 tablespoon black beans, chopped
½ teaspoon chopped garlic
½ teaspoon salt
1 tablespoon light soy sauce
1 tablespoon dry sherry

Combine filling ingredients. Cut each melon in half lengthways. Scoop out seeds and pulp with a spoon. Place filling in centre of melon.

Arrange melon pieces cut side up in a heatproof dish. Steam 20 minutes. Serve hot.

Alternatively, remove ends from melons. Scoop out seeds and pulp. Fill melons with filling and steam 20 minutes. Cut into 2 cm slices.

Serves 8

STIR-FRIED SWEET AND SOUR VEGETABLES

1 green capsicum
1 medium onion
2 stalks celery
2 carrots
2 tablespoons oil
1 clove garlic, crushed
2 thin slices fresh ginger root, finely chopped
75 g shredded canned bamboo shoots
3 tablespoons vinegar
2 tablespoons sugar
1 tablespoon sherry
2 tablespoons chicken stock
1 tablespoon cornflour blended with 2 tablespoons water

Remove membrane and seeds from capsicum and cut into 5 cm long diamond shapes. Peel onion, halve lengthways and cut each half into 1 cm wide strips lengthways. Cut celery in 5 cm pieces diagonally. Cut carrots in a rolling cut, diagonally into 4 cm pieces. Parboil 3–4 minutes.

Heat oil in a wok. Add garlic and ginger, and stir for 1 minute. Add vegetables and stir-fry over high heat about 2 minutes. Add vinegar, sugar, sherry and chicken stock and bring to the boil. Stir in blended cornflour and water to thicken.

Serves 4

ASPARAGUS IN THE SNOW

500 g fresh green asparagus, tough ends removed
1 slice fresh ginger root
1 tablespoon dry sherry
2 tablespoons vegetable stock
2 egg whites
1 tablespoon cornflour
1 cup seasoned vegetable stock (250 mL)

Place asparagus, ginger, sherry and stock into pan. Cook over high heat 3–4 minutes until crispy tender. Place asparagus on a serving platter, reserving cooking liquid.

To make sauce, beat egg whites with asparagus cooking liquid. Blend corn flour with seasoned stock. Heat until thickened. Whisk 2 tablespoons heated thickened stock into egg mixture. Whisk egg mixture into remaining sauce. Serve hot.

Serves 4

EIGHT MINUTE VEGETABLES

3 tablespoons oil
1 clove garlic, crushed
4 slices fresh ginger root, finely chopped
½ Chinese cabbage, sliced
1 small green capsicum, shredded
250 g broccoli, trimmed into florets
125 g bean sprouts, washed and shaken dry
¾ cup chicken stock (180 mL)
2 teaspoons soy sauce
1 teaspoon brown sugar

In a large wok heat oil. Add garlic and ginger and stir-fry 1 minute. Add cabbage, green capsicum and broccoli and stir-fry 3 minutes.

Add bean sprouts and stir-fry 1 minute. Stir in stock, soy sauce and sugar. Cook for 3 minutes and serve.

Serves 4

VERMICELLI AND VEGETABLES

4 Chinese mushrooms, soaked in warm water 20 minutes
⅓ cup oil (80 mL)
2 onions, cut in wedges
1 garlic clove, crushed
1 green capsicum, sliced
1 red capsicum, sliced
3 stalks celery, sliced
250 g bean sprouts
8 canned water chestnuts, halved
¾ cup pineapple juice (180 mL)
1 tablespoon white vinegar
1 teaspoon chilli sauce
1 tablespoon oyster sauce
1½ tablespoons soy sauce
250 g vermicelli noodles, soaked in warm water for 20 minutes and drained

Drain mushrooms and squeeze dry. Discard stalks and slice caps.

Heat oil in a wok. Add onions, garlic, capsicums and celery, and stir fry for 3–4 minutes.

Stir in mushrooms, bean sprouts and chestnuts. Pour over pineapple juice, vinegar and sauces. Bring to the boil.

Stir in vermicelli, reduce heat and simmer, stirring occasionally for 3–5 minutes until vermicelli are tender.

Serves 4

Steamed Bitter Melons (left) and Vermicelli and Vegetables (right)

Braised Vegetables

EGGPLANT WITH BEAN CURD AND BASIL

1 tablespoon vegetable oil
1 teaspoon chopped garlic
250 g firm bean curd, cut in 2 cm dice
1 medium eggplant, peeled and cut in
  2 cm dice
4 ripe tomatoes, peeled and quartered
½ teaspoon sugar
¼ teaspoon dried basil
½ teaspoon salt
¼ teaspoon pepper
½ cup vegetable stock (125 mL)

Heat oil in a wok. Lightly fry garlic and bean curd. Add eggplant, tomatoes, sugar, basil, salt, pepper and stock. Bring to the boil, then simmer gently until eggplant is tender. The mixture may be thickened slightly with cornflour if preferred.

Serves 6

BRAISED VEGETABLES

2 tablespoons oil
1 teaspoon sesame oil
1 clove garlic, crushed
1 teaspoon finely chopped fresh
  ginger root
500 g prepared mixed vegetables
½ cup hot water (125 mL)
1 tablespoon oyster sauce
1 tablespoon soy sauce
2 teaspoons cornflour blended with
  1 tablespoon water

In a wok heat oil and add sesame oil, garlic and ginger. Add vegetables and stir-fry 2 minutes. Add hot water, oyster and soy sauces. Simmer 4 minutes.

Push vegetables to one side of wok, add blended cornflour and water and stir until sauce thickens. Fork vegetables through sauce and serve with boiled rice.

Serves 4

Stir-fried Broccoli and Bean Curd in Oyster Sauce

STIR-FRIED BROCCOLI AND BEAN CURD IN OYSTER SAUCE

500 g broccoli
2 tablespoons oil
fresh ginger root, sliced
1 clove garlic, finely chopped
¼ cup canned bamboo shoots,
  shredded
2 cakes bean curd, cut in 1 cm cubes
2 tablespoons oyster sauce
1 tablespoon soy sauce
½ cup chicken stock (125 mL)
1 teaspoon cornflour blended with
  2 tablespoons water

Cut off florets from broccoli stems. Discard tough ends and cut wide stems in half lengthways. Cut in 2 cm pieces diagonally. Parboil in a large quantity of salted water 3–4 minutes. Drain and rinse broccoli under cold running water. Cool completely.

Heat oil in a wok until very hot. Add ginger and garlic. Stir-fry 1 minute until ginger is lightly browned. Discard ginger and garlic. Add drained broccoli and stir-fry 1 minute. Add bamboo shoots, bean curd, sauces and chicken stock. Bring to the boil, reduce heat, cover and simmer for 2 minutes. Stir in blended cornflour and water to thicken the sauce.

Serves 4

Stuffed Bean Curd
Cut bean curd cakes in half.

Carefully stuff cakes with filling.

Steam cakes in a shallow heatproof dish.

Stuffed Bean Curd

STIR-FRIED BEAN SPROUTS

375 g bean sprouts
2 tablespoons oil
1 thin slice fresh ginger root, finely
   chopped
½ green capsicum, sliced
½ medium onion, cut in wedges
12 shallots, sliced
2 thin slices ham, shredded
2 tablespoons chicken stock combined
   with
½ tablespoon sherry

Pour boiling water over bean sprouts and
let stand 20 seconds.

Refresh in cold running water, drain
and dry. Heat oil in a wok. Add ginger and
stir-fry 30 seconds. Add capsicum, onion
and shallots and stir-fry 1 ½ minutes. Add
bean sprouts and ham and stir-fry 30
seconds. Add combined stock and
sherry and bring to the boil. Remove from
heat and serve.

Serves 4

STUFFED BEAN CURD

6 cakes bean curd
1 ½ tablespoons oil
1 thin slice fresh ginger root, finely
   chopped
1 clove garlic, crushed
2 stalks celery, or 6 leaves cabbage or
   other seasonal green vegetable, cut
   into 4 cm diamonds
¾ cup chicken stock (180 mL)
2 tablespoons soy sauce
1 tablespoon sherry
1 tablespoon cornflour blended with
   2 tablespoons water

FILLING

125 g lean pork, minced
6 shallots, minced
2 water chestnuts, minced
½ tablespoon soy sauce
1 tablespoon sherry
1 egg yolk

Cut bean curd cakes in half. Make a
pocket in each half to contain filling, tak-
ing care not to break bean curd. In a
bowl, combine filling ingredients. Stuff
bean curd carefully with this mixture.
Place bean curd in a shallow heatproof
dish and steam for about 25 minutes.

About 5 minutes before the steaming is
completed, heat oil in a wok. Add ginger
and garlic. Stir-fry 1 minute until golden
brown. Discard ginger and garlic.
Increase heat, add celery and stir-fry for
1 minute. Add chicken stock, soy sauce
and sherry.

Reduce heat, cover and continue
cooking for 1 ½ minutes. Stir blended
cornflour and water into vegetables.
Cook 30 seconds until thickened.
Remove dish with bean curd from the
steamer. Serve with Chinese Rice (see
recipe).

Serves 4

65

ALL OCCASION RICE AND NOODLES

Everyone who loves Chinese food can enjoy the extraordinary variety of noodle and rice dishes, created as the staple food of China. The crunchy texture of rice, and the smooth texture of noodles, with their relatively bland taste, make the perfect accompaniment to other, spicier flavours.

POTATO NESTS OR BASKETS

500 g grated potato
2 tablespoons cornflour
salt and pepper
oil, for frying

Combine potato, cornflour and seasoning. Dip basket moulds or wire strainers into hot oil. Place 3–4 tablespoons potato mixture into the larger basket. Arrange to cover surface of basket.

Place smaller basket on top. Holding the handles of both baskets together, dip into hot oil to cover.

When the potato sets, the smaller mould can be removed. Continue cooking until crisp and golden.

Use for serving deep- or stir-fried food.

Makes 1

FRESH EGG NOODLE BASKETS

60–90 g fresh egg noodles
oil, for frying

Line basket moulds with fresh egg noodle. Cook as for Potato Nests (see recipe).

Makes 4–6

VERMICELLI NESTS OR BASKETS

30 g vermicelli noodles
oil, for frying

Cut vermicelli noodles into 2.5 cm lengths. Line large mould and fry as for Potato Nests (see recipe).

Makes 1

THREE JEWELLED CHICKEN IN NOODLE BASKETS

vermicelli noodle baskets (see recipe)

FILLING

200 g boneless chicken breast, thinly sliced
1 teaspoon cornflour
2 teaspoons egg white
2 tablespoons vegetable oil
1 ½ tablespoons ginger in syrup, sliced
100 g canned lychees
100 g canned loquats

SAUCE

1 tablespoon cornflour
2 tablespoons light soy sauce
2 tablespoons white vinegar
2 tablespoons sugar
6 tablespoons lychee juice

Combine chicken, cornflour and egg white in a bowl. Heat oil in a wok. Stir-fry chicken until white. Add ginger, lychees and loquats.

Blend sauce ingredients. Heat in a pan, stir to form sauce and thicken.

Serve mixture evenly in noodle baskets.

Serves 6 individual baskets or 2 large baskets

Fresh Egg Noodle Baskets in the making (above) and Three Jewelled Chicken in Noodle Baskets (below)

CONGEE ROAST DUCK

¾ cup uncooked rice (150 g)
1.5 litres water
2 small dried scallops, 2 tablespoons
    dried prawns or 1½ teaspoons salt
1 small piece dried tangerine or orange
    peel
¼ roast duck, cut into bite-sized pieces
    (see Note)
1 tablespoon sherry
2 tablespoons sliced shallots

Place rice and water in a pan. Add scallops and tangerine peel. Bring to the boil over high heat. Reduce heat, cover and simmer for 45 minutes.

Add roast duck and sherry. Cover and simmer for at least 1 hour, stirring occasionally and adding some water if the congee becomes too thick.

Remove tangerine peel and dried scallops, if desired. Top with shallots and serve.

Note: Roast duck should be available from speciality Chinese shops, or you may prepare your own. Marinate duck pieces in Char Sui marinade and cook as for Char Sui (see recipe).

Serves 4

CRISPY NOODLES

350 g egg noodles (preferably fresh)
2 tablespoons oil
1 onion, shredded
½ bunch celery, shredded
250 g chicken or pork, shredded
1 tablespoon soy sauce
oil, for deep-frying

Cook noodles as directed in Noodle Cooking recipe. Drain, rinse well and set aside. After about 10 minutes, turn out noodles onto a tray and separate them with chopsticks or a fork.

Heat oil in a wok and stir-fry vegetables and meat together for about 5–6 minutes. While still crisp, season with soy sauce and keep warm.

Put noodles into a strainer, heat the oil for deep-frying and plunge strainer into the oil; fry until noodles are crisp then drain on absorbent kitchen paper. Turn onto serving dish and add meat and vegetable sauce.

Serves 4

Crispy Noodles

Separate cooked noodles with chopsticks.

Stir-fry vegetables and meat together.

Deep-fry noodles in hot oil until crisp.

Pork Fried Rice

BARBECUED PORK CHOW MEIN

2 tablespoons vegetable oil
1 teaspoon chopped fresh ginger root
1 teaspoon chopped garlic
250 g Chinese barbecued pork (Char Sui)
4 Chinese mushrooms, soaked in warm water 20 minutes and sliced
60 g carrot, sliced and parboiled
200 g broccoli florets, blanched
60 g bamboo shoot, sliced
125 g bean sprouts, root removed
½ cup stock (125 mL)
2 tablespoons light soy sauce
1 tablespoon dry sherry
1 teaspoon sugar
1 tablespoon cornflour blended with 2 tablespoons water
250 g soft fried noodles (see recipe)

Heat oil in a wok. Add ginger, garlic, pork and stir-fry 1–2 minutes. Add vegetables, stock, soy sauce, sherry and sugar. Simmer covered for 2 minutes. Stir in blended cornflour and water to thicken. Serve over hot noodles.

Serves 6

PORK FRIED RICE

1 ½ cups uncooked rice (300 g)
3 tablespoons oil
2 eggs, lightly beaten
1 clove garlic, bruised
1 slice fresh ginger root, roughly chopped
6 shallots, cut in 1 cm pieces
250 g Chinese barbecued pork (Char Sui)
3 tablespoons soy sauce

Cook the rice as described in Chinese Rice recipe. Heat 1 tablespoon oil in a wok. Pour in beaten eggs to form a flat omelette; cook for 2 minutes. When bottom is set, flip over and cook for further 2 minutes. Remove from heat, roll up Swiss-roll style and cut into thin strips.

Heat remaining oil in wok, add garlic and ginger and cook until browned, drain and discard. Add shallots and rice. Stir-fry 2–3 minutes. Add Char Sui and soy sauce, and stir-fry 1 minute. Add a little water if too dry. Spoon rice into a serving dish and garnish with egg strips.

Serves 4

FRIED RICE WITH BEEF AND ALMONDS

250 g lean steak, thinly sliced and shredded
1 tablespoon soy sauce
1 tablespoon cornflour
3 tablespoons vegetable oil
1 large onion, cut in fine shreds
1 medium capsicum, cut in fine shreds
½ teaspoon salt
2 cups hot steamed rice (500 g)
125 g almonds, toasted

GARNISH

shallot shreds
extra toasted almonds

Combine steak, soy sauce and cornflour. Heat oil in a wok and add steak mixture. Stir-fry 2 minutes. Add onion, capsicum and salt. Stir-fry 1 minute. Add rice and almonds, stir-frying to blend ingredients. This step can be done off the heat.

Place mixture into an oiled ring mould. Press down firmly. Turn out onto round serving plate, garnish and serve.

Serves 6

69

RICE

Rice is one of the best sources of nutrition and nourishment around the world. Brown rice is better value than white rice, but both can be useful in our diets, as they are:

- high in protein and dietary fibre
- high in vitamins and minerals — calcium, iron, thiamine, riboflavin and niacin
- low in fat, salt and sugar
- cholesterol-free

On the question of how much to use, the general rule is ½ cup (100 g) raw rice per person. If steaming, allow 2 cups water (500 mL) for the first cup of rice, and 1½ cups water (375 mL) for each additional cup of rice.

CHINESE RICE

2½ cups uncooked rice (500 g)
water

Wash rice in cold water until water runs clear. Place rice in saucepan and cover with water to 2.5 cm above rice level. Bring to the boil, reduce heat to medium and continue cooking, uncovered, until water evaporates (air bubble holes will form through rice).

When water has evaporated, place lid on saucepan and continue cooking for 7 minutes on low heat. Do not stir or lift lid during last 7 minutes of cooking. If not using immediately, leave in covered pan.

Serves 4–6

STEAMED WHITE RICE

uncooked rice, allowing ½ cup per person (100 g)
water

Rinse rice with cold water several times. Place rice in a medium-sized saucepan and cover with cold water to 2 cm above the rice. Bring to the boil. Stir once and cook uncovered until air bubble holes form. Reduce heat to low. Cover and steam for 20 minutes.

Remove from heat and allow to stand covered 5 minutes. Stir rice grains with a fork to loosen, avoiding cutting through grains.

Steamed rice will remain hot in the saucepan for over 30 minutes. During this time several stir-fry dishes can be prepared.

To serve rice, place into individual rice bowls and press down firmly with a spoon. Turn out onto serving plates and top each with shallot flowers.

For fried rice, cook in advance. Spread rice onto a tray and refrigerate until required. Cooked rice will freeze and defrost well.

FRIED RICE

2 cups cold cooked rice (500 g)
3 eggs, beaten lightly
2 tablespoons vegetable oil
90 g cooked prawn meat, cut in 5 mm dice (optional)
2 rashers cooked bacon, drained, cut in 5 mm dice or 125 g Char Sui (see recipe)
2 shallots, cut in 5 mm dice
1 tablespoon light soy sauce
¼ teaspoon sesame oil
salt and pepper

Fold beaten eggs through rice.

Heat wok. Add oil by pouring it around the rims. This seals the wok and heats the oil quickly. Add rice and stir-fry over high heat; after a few minutes the grains will separate. Add prawns and bacon. Stir-fry 1 minute. Add remaining ingredients and stir-fry to blend flavours. Serve rice in a warm Chinese bowl to retain heat during serving.

Serves 6

STEAMED BROWN RICE

2 cups uncooked brown rice (400 g)
3½ cups cold water (875 mL)

Rinse rice in a sieve under cold water. Place rice and measured water into large saucepan. Cook uncovered over high heat until boiling. Stir once. Reduce heat to low and cook covered 25–30 minutes. Let stand covered for 5 minutes before removing lid. The water should be completely absorbed. Loosen grains with a fork. Serve hot.

For fried rice, turn rice out onto tray and allow to cool. Chill in refrigerator before frying.

Serves 4

COMBINATION SEAFOOD CHOW MEIN

250 g crisp fried fresh egg noodles (see recipe)
125 g prawn meat, deveined
125 g scallops
125 g prepared squid
125 g sliced fish fillets
½ teaspoon chopped fresh ginger root
2 tablespoons cornflour
2 tablespoons light soy sauce
2 tablespoons sherry
4 tablespoons oil
½ teaspoon salt
4 stalks Chinese cabbage, cut in 2.5 cm pieces
1 cup sliced bamboo shoots (150 g)
180 g straw mushrooms, sliced lengthways

Cook noodles according to Crisp Fried Fresh Egg Noodles recipe. Arrange noodles on serving platter and keep warm.

Combine seafood, ginger, cornflour, soy sauce and sherry, toss to coat.

Heat 2 tablespoons oil. Add seafood and stir-fry 2–3 minutes. Remove from pan.

Heat remaining oil. Add salt and Chinese cabbage stalks, and stir-fry 1 minute. Add cabbage leaves, bamboo shoots and mushrooms. Cover and cook 2 minutes.

Return seafood to reheat. Serve over crisp noodles.

Serves 6–8

NOODLES

In China, noodles are traditionally the food of the north. They are made mainly from grains, but sometimes also from seaweed or the starch of mung peas. Noodles are almost always made in thin threads, but there is considerable variety in texture, thickness and width. They can be boiled, steamed, soft-fried, deep-fried and used in soups. These days, they are often available from larger supermarkets and delicatessens, as well as from Asian foodstores and Chinese grocers.

SOFT-FRIED NOODLES

Dried long-life egg and eggless noodles are available in various packs. The noodles can be thin, round or flat and come in 50 g bundles, usually 6–8 bundles per packet. Dried noodles are also available flavoured e.g. chicken, shrimp, beef and curry.

FRIED NOODLES WITH CHICKEN AND VEGETABLES

250 g fresh egg noodles
oil, for deep-frying
1 whole chicken breast, skinned and
*   boned*
250 g green (uncooked) prawns, shelled
1 clove garlic, crushed
1 piece bamboo shoot, shredded
6 Chinese mushrooms, soaked in warm
*   water for 20 minutes and sliced*
125 g vegetables (e.g. celery, shallots,
*   beans), cut into matchsticks*
½ cup stock (125 mL)
½ teaspoon cornflour
1 tablespoon soy sauce
pinch five spice powder

Divide noodles into four portions. Deep-fry each portion in hot oil until golden brown. Drain on absorbent kitchen paper.

Cut chicken meat into strips. Heat wok, add 1 tablespoon vegetable oil and stir-fry chicken and prawns with garlic. Add shredded bamboo shoot, mushrooms and vegetables and stir-fry for a further 5 minutes.

Pour in combined stock, cornflour, soy sauce and five spice powder and simmer for 5 minutes.

To serve, place noodles on a plate and spoon over chicken and vegetables. Serve immediately.

Serves 4

Fried Noodles with Chicken and Vegetables

TO COOK DRY NOODLES

1–1.25 litres water
1 teaspoon salt
250 g dried noodles
vegetable or sesame oil

TO SOFT-FRY NOODLES

4 tablespoons vegetable oil
½ teaspoon salt

Bring water to the boil. Add salt, then noodles. Stir with chopsticks to loosen each bundle. Cooking should be completed in 3–5 minutes. Do not overcook; remember noodles will also be fried. Drain well, rinse in cold water. Drain and spread loosely on a tray. Sprinkle with a little oil and refrigerate for 2 hours before frying.

Heat oil with salt. When very hot, carefully add cooked noodles. Use tongs or chopsticks to loosen noodles. Reduce heat and fry noodles for 2 minutes. Turn noodles over and cook another 2 minutes. The noodles should be lightly brown and crisp on the outside. Serves 4

NOODLE COOKING

2–2.5 litres water
2 teaspoons salt
1 tablespoon oil
500 g noodles

Bring water, salt and oil to boil over high heat. Add noodles gradually so that the water maintains the boil.

Boil uncovered for 6 minutes for dried noodles and 5 minutes for fresh noodles, stirring occasionally. Test noodles to see whether they are cooked. If still firm, continue cooking for 1 or 2 more minutes.

Drain noodles and rinse under cold water. If they are to be used right away, drop into boiling water until just heated through. Drain and use as needed. If to be used later, spread out in a large bowl and sprinkle with a little oil to prevent sticking. Reheat as directed above.

Serves 4 as an accompaniment.

CRISP-FRIED FRESH EGG NOODLES

Fresh egg noodles are available from Chinese foodstores in the refrigerated section. When deep-fried they become very crisp and are served with various toppings. They are known as Chow Mein, chow meaning fried, mein meaning noodles.

250 g fresh egg noodles
1½ cups oil, for deep-frying (375 mL)

Heat oil in a wok. Test temperature with 1 stream of noodle. If it crisps up quickly, the oil is the correct temperature.

Cook the noodles in two batches. Separate the noodles with both hands, then carefully lower them into the oil. Cook 2 minutes, turn over with tongs and continue cooking until crisp and golden.

Arrange on serving platter and add a stir-fried topping.

Serves 2–4

SWEET, SOUR OR SALTY — SAUCES AND DIPS

Many sauces are available bottled or canned from your local supermarket, still more from foodstores in Chinatowns. It's fun, however, to experiment and make your own sauces and dips, as spicy as you like. They take very little time to prepare, and make all the difference to even the simplest bowl of rice.

SWEET AND SOUR SAUCE

½ cup sugar (125 g)
½ cup vinegar (125 mL)
4–5 tablespoons light soy sauce
1 tablespoon dark soy sauce (optional)
2 tablespoons sherry
1 ½ tablespoons cornflour blended with
   ½ cup water (125 mL)

In a saucepan, combine sugar, vinegar, light soy sauce, dark soy sauce and sherry. Bring to the boil and stir in the blended cornflour and water to thicken. Use as directed in recipes.

Makes about 1 ½ cups (375 mL)

PLUM SAUCE

10 fresh plums, pitted and finely
   chopped
¼ cup dried apricots (35 g), soaked in
   warm water 1 hour and finely chopped
1 teaspoon chilli sauce
1 teaspoon salt
2 tablespoons water
½ cup sugar (125 g)
½ cup vinegar (125 mL)

Place plums and apricots in a wok. Add chilli sauce, salt and water. Bring to the boil and simmer gently 15 minutes. Add a little more water if the mixture becomes too dry.

Stir in sugar and vinegar and simmer 20–30 minutes until the sauce reaches a chutney-like consistency. Pour sauce into a sterilised jar, cover and refrigerate when cool. This sauce will keep several months.

Makes about 1 cup (250 mL)

PEPPER AND SALT MIX

3 tablespoons salt
2 tablespoons Szechuan peppercorns or
   crushed peppercorns

Heat a wok until very hot. Add salt and peppercorns, reduce the heat and stir 5–6 minutes or until salt is light brown.

Remove from wok and crush peppercorns in a mortar and pestle. Sift through a sieve. Store pepper and salt mix in a tightly covered jar.

Makes 100 g

SWEET AND SOUR FRUITY SAUCE

½ cup sugar (125 g)
½ cup vinegar (125 mL)
2 tablespoons soy sauce
2 tablespoons sherry
3 tablespoons tomato sauce
2 tablespoons cornflour blended with
   ½ cup pineapple juice

In a saucepan, combine sugar, vinegar, soy sauce, sherry and tomato sauce. Bring to the boil and add blended cornflour and pineapple juice, stirring constantly until the sauce is thickened. Use as directed in recipes.

Makes about 1 ½ cups (375 mL)

Top row left to right: Dip for Mussels, Pepper and Salt Mix in mortar and pestle, and in jar, Ginger Soy Dip, Oyster Sauce; bottom row left to right: Plum Sauce, Sherry Soy Dip, Sweet and Sour Sauce, Sweet and Sour Fruity Sauce, Sweet and Sour Ginger Sauce

OYSTER SAUCE

If bottled oyster sauce is not available, a fair substitute can be made following this recipe. Do not use smoked oysters or any other flavoured preparation.

250 g bottled oysters
1 tablespoon water
1 teaspoon salt
soy sauce
½ tablespoon dark soy sauce

Drain oysters and reserve liquid. Mince the oysters or chop finely and place in a saucepan. Add water and reserved oyster liquid and bring to the boil. Reduce heat, cover and simmer about 10 minutes.

Remove from heat, add salt and cool completely. Force the mixture through a fine sieve into saucepan. Measure the liquid, adding 2 tablespoons soy sauce to each ½ cup (125 mL).

Add dark soy sauce and bring to boil. Reduce heat and simmer gently about 7 minutes.

Cool to room temperature and pour into a sterilised jar. Seal and store in the refrigerator. This sauce can be kept for several weeks.

Makes about 1½–2 cups (375–500 mL)

GINGER-SOY DIP

2 tablespoons oil
1 tablespoon finely chopped shallots, white part only
½ teaspoon finely grated fresh ginger root
4 tablespoons soy sauce

Heat oil in a wok. Add shallots and ginger root and stir-fry 30 seconds. Add soy sauce and remove from heat.

Makes about 150 mL

SWEET AND SOUR GINGER SAUCE

½ cup sugar (125 g)
6 cm slice fresh ginger root, finely chopped
½ cup vinegar (125 mL)
½ cup pineapple juice (125 mL)
1 tablespoon sherry
1½ tablespoons cornflour blended with ⅓ cup water (80 mL)
125 g Chinese pickle, finely sliced

In a saucepan, combine sugar, ginger, vinegar, pineapple juice and sherry. Bring to the boil and stir in blended cornflour and water to thicken. Stir in Chinese pickle. Use as directed in recipes.

Makes about 2 cups (500 mL)

DIP FOR MUSSELS

1 teaspoon chopped fresh ginger root
2 tablespoons light soy sauce
1 tablespoon dry sherry
¼ teaspoon chilli sauce
few drops sesame oil

Blend and serve in a dip sauce bowl, with fresh, cooked mussels.

Makes about ¼ cup (60 mL).

SHERRY-SOY DIP

2 tablespoons sherry
2 tablespoons soy sauce
¼ teaspoon sugar

Combine all ingredients and stir together until the sugar has dissolved. Goes well with chicken dishes.

Makes ⅓ cup (80 mL)

LIGHT AND LOW-CHOLESTEROL

Chinese cooking is a healthy cuisine to start with; these recipes are even better. By dispensing with added salt, sugar and fat, and using ingredients like low-salt soy sauce and vegetable stock, dishes such as Scallop Satay, Veal Spring Rolls and Fish Cocktails with Honey Sauce can be recommended for anyone with an interest in delicious food.

STEAMED DIM SUM

100 g eggless wonton skins
1—2 tablespoons peas
lettuce leaves, to steam

FILLING

250 g chicken, steamed and finely
    chopped
250 g firm white fish fillets, finely
    chopped
1 shallot, finely cut
4 tablespoons chopped water
    chestnuts
4 Chinese mushrooms, soaked in
    warm water 20 minutes and finely
    chopped
1 tablespoon salt-reduced soy sauce
pinch pepper

DIP SAUCE

2 tablespoons salt-reduced soy sauce
1 tablespoon white vinegar

Mix all filling ingredients together. Place 2-3 teaspoons filling in the centre of each skin. Gather edges around filling and press so that filling comes up to the edge of each skin. Place a pea on top of filling. The dim sum should have a flat base and stand upright.

Place a few lettuce leaves into a bamboo steamer. Arrange dim sum on top with enough space between them so they don't touch. Steam covered 20 minutes. Serve with sauce.

To make dip sauce, combine ingredients in a small bowl.

Serve 4–6

BEEF FILLET WITH SWEET AND SOUR SAUCE

500 g fillet steak, cut in 1 cm dice
1 tablespoon salt-reduced soy sauce
¼ teaspoon five spice powder

SWEET AND SOUR SAUCE

1 cup unsweetened pineapple juice
    (250 mL)
1 tablespoon sugar
1 tablespoon white vinegar
1 tablespoon cornflour
1 tablespoon dry sherry
1 cup beef consomme (250 mL)
½ green capsicum, cut in 1 cm dice
¼ carrot, parboiled, cut in 1 cm dice
50 g unsweetened pineapple pieces
90 g diced Chinese mixed pickles

Combine diced steak with soy sauce and five spice powder and marinate 15 minutes. Heat a non-stick pan, add one-quarter of the steak and stir-fry 3–4 minutes. Remove from pan. Repeat with remaining beef. Set aside and keep warm.

Bring pineapple juice, sugar and vinegar to the boil. Blend cornflour, sherry and stock to a paste. Stir into pineapple juice to thicken. Add vegetables, simmer 3 minutes. Add diced steak to heat through. Serve at once.

Serves 4–6

Beef Fillet with Sweet and Sour Sauce
(above) and Steamed Dim Sum (below)

COLD SUMMER NOODLES

500 g eggless, curry flavoured noodles
1.5 litres vegetable stock
250 g chicken breast, steamed and
    shredded
250 g fresh bean sprouts, roots
    removed and blanched
1 telegraph cucumber, cut in half
    lengthways, and shredded
1 teaspoon chopped garlic
3 tablespoons vinegar
3 tablespoons salt-reduced soy sauce

Cook noodles in boiling stock 4 minutes. Drain and cool, discarding stock.

Combine chicken, bean sprouts and cucumber. Add garlic, vinegar and soy sauce. Add to noodles, toss to blend. Serve chilled.

Serves 4

STIR-FRIED BEEF WITH CHILLI BEAN SAUCE

250 g fillet steak, thinly sliced
1 tablespoon dry sherry
¼ cup beef consomme (60 mL)
1 teaspoon chopped garlic
1 tablespoon chilli bean sauce
1 large onion, cut into eighths
2 teaspoons cornflour
1 teaspoon salt-reduced soy sauce
3 tablespoons vegetable stock or
    water

Combine sliced steak and sherry. Heat a non-stick pan, add beef and stir-fry 2 minutes. Remove from pan and set aside.

Reheat pan, add consomme, garlic, chilli bean sauce and onion, and simmer covered 2 minutes. Return steak to pan. Blend cornflour with soy sauce and stock. Stir in to thicken and serve at once.   Serves 4

Spaghetti Squash with Peking Sauce

BRAISED MIXED VEGETABLES

½ cup vegetable stock (125 mL)
1 teaspoon chopped fresh ginger root
½ teaspoon chopped garlic
½ teaspoon sugar
125 g broccoli florets
1 large onion, cut into eighths
125 g snake beans, cut into 2.5 cm
    lengths
125 g bamboo shoots, sliced
125 g straw mushrooms
1 tablespoon salt-reduced soy sauce
1 tablespoon oyster sauce
1 tablespoon dry sherry
2 teaspoons cornflour

Bring stock to the boil in a pan. Add ginger, garlic, sugar, broccoli, onion and beans. Cover, and cook on high heat 3–4 minutes. Add bamboo shoots and straw mushrooms.

Blend soy and oyster sauces with sherry and cornflour. Stir into vegetable mixture to thicken slightly. Serve at once.

Serves 4–6

STIR-FRIED CHICKEN WITH BEAN SPROUTS

¼ cup vegetable stock (60 mL)
125 g fresh chicken breast, skinned
    and shredded
500 g bean sprouts, root removed
2 teaspoons cornflour
2 teaspoons dry sherry
¼ teaspoon sugar
1 tablespoon salt-reduced soy sauce

Heat stock in a non-stick pan. Add chicken strips and stir-fry 3 minutes. Add bean sprouts. Cook covered 2 minutes. Blend cornflour, sherry, sugar and soy sauce. Stir in to thicken. Serve at once.

Garnish with shallot shreds.

Serves 4

SPAGHETTI SQUASH WITH PEKING SAUCE

500–750 g spaghetti squash in one
    piece
1 ½ cups vegetable stock (375 mL)

SAUCE

250 g lean veal, minced
2 teaspoons dry sherry
½ cup onion, finely chopped
1 tablespoon canned yellow bean
    sauce (see Glossary)
2 tablespoons salt-reduced soy sauce
1 tablespoon hoisin sauce
1 ½ cups seasoned vegetable stock
    (375 mL)
1 tablespoon finely chopped fresh
    coriander

To prepare squash, leave skin on and remove seeds with a spoon. Place stock in a saucepan. Stand squash cut side up in saucepan, cover, and bring liquid to the boil. Simmer 20 minutes until squash is tender.

Remove squash and scrape out flesh in long strands from skin. Place on a warm serving platter.

To make sauce, combine veal with sherry and onion in a non-stick pan. Stir-fry until veal loses its pink colour. Add bean paste, soy and hoisin sauces with stock and simmer 20 minutes.

The sauce can be thickened slightly if desired. Serve poured over spaghetti squash and garnish with fresh coriander.

Serves 4

CHICKEN AND VEGETABLE SATAY

250 g chicken breast, skin removed, cut
    in 2 cm dice
1 tablespoon salt-reduced soy sauce
1 medium onion, quartered
¼ red capsicum, cut into 2 cm dice
8 button mushrooms
4 long bamboo satay sticks, soaked in
    water to prevent burning
¼ cup orange juice (60 mL)

Combine chicken with soy sauce and let marinate 15 minutes. Thread chicken, onion, capsicum and mushrooms onto satay sticks. Place on a sheet of foil and brush with orange juice.

Grill under medium heat until chicken is white. Baste with orange juice frequently to prevent drying out. Serve hot with brown rice.

Serves 4

*Stir-fried Beef with Chilli Bean Sauce
(above) and Chicken and Vegetable
Satay (below)*

ESPECIALLY VEGETARIAN

Delicious meat-free recipes are sprinkled throughout this book, but here are dishes with interesting alternative ingredients such as bean curd and mock duck, available at your local health food stores and larger supermarkets. Try Barbecued Bean Curd or Tossed Rice Noodles with Chop Suey to whet the appetite.

STIR-FRIED BEAN CURD WITH SZECHUAN SAUCE

3 tablespoons vegetable oil
¼ teaspoon salt
2 shallots, cut into 2 cm lengths
500 g firm bean curd, cut in 2 cm dice
4 tablespoons Szechuan sauce (see recipe)

Heat oil in a wok. Add salt, white of shallot and bean curd cubes. Stir-fry gently to heat through. Add Szechuan sauce and simmer 3 minutes. Stir in shallot greens and serve.

Serves 6-8

NOODLE SOUP WITH QUAIL EGGS

1–2.5 litres water
250 g fresh egg noodles
¾ teaspoon salt
2 teaspoons soy sauce
1 teaspoon peanut oil
few drops sesame oil
pinch white pepper
12 quail eggs, boiled and shelled
3 shallots, finely cut
2 litres boiling vegetable stock

Bring water to the boil. Add salt and noodles. Cook 3–5 minutes until just tender. Drain, then rinse in cold water. Drain again.

Place noodles in a large tureen. Add soy sauce, peanut and sesame oils and pepper. Toss well to mix.

Arrange eggs and shallots over noodles. Pour over stock and serve at once with the sauce of your choice. Quail eggs taste particularly delicious with Szechuan sauce (see recipe).

Serves 6

BEAN SPROUT SALAD

500 g soy bean sprouts
2 tablespoons light soy sauce
1 tablespoon white vinegar
1 teaspoon sugar
½ teaspoon sesame oil
250 g snow pea sprouts (see Note)
1 bean curd cake, cut in julienne strips
¼ red capsicum, cut in julienne strips

Blanch soy bean sprouts in boiling water for 1 minute. Refresh in cold water and drain well.

Combine soy sauce, vinegar, sugar and sesame oil in a bowl, add soy bean and snow pea sprouts. Toss to coat with dressing. Cover and chill 20 minutes.

Arrange salad on serving platter. Garnish with bean curd and capsicum.

Note: Snow pea sprouts are available from most Chinese foodstores and some groceries in clear plastic packs.

Serves 8

SZECHUAN SAUCE

2 tablespoons vegetable oil
3 red chillies, chopped
2 teaspoons chopped ginger root
2 teaspoons chopped garlic
½ medium onion, chopped
2 tablespoons dry sherry
4 tablespoons sugar
4 tablespoons tomato sauce
4 tablespoons white vinegar

To make the sauce, heat oil in a pan. Add chillies, ginger, garlic and onion. Fry until tender. Add sherry, sugar, tomato sauce and vinegar, and simmer 10–15 minutes.

Makes approximately 1 cup (250 mL)

Noodle Soup with Quail Eggs (above), Stir-fried Bean Curd with Szechuan Sauce (centre) and Bean Sprout Salad (below)

CRUNCHY OMELETTE IN A NEST

2 tablespoons vegetable oil
1 medium onion, finely shredded
2 stalks celery, finely chopped
½ red capsicum, finely chopped
5 fresh mushrooms, thickly sliced
125 g bean sprouts, root removed
salt and pepper
6 eggs, beaten
1 shallot, finely chopped
1 tablespoon chopped cashew nuts
1 large potato nest (see recipe)

Heat oil in a wok. Add onion, celery and capsicum, and stir-fry 2 minutes. Add mushrooms, bean sprouts and seasonings and stir-fry 1 minute. Pour in eggs. Fold into vegetables until mixture sets. Turn over and cook on the other side, about 1 minute.

Remove and cut into strips. Place into potato nest. Sprinkle with shallots and cashews, and serve at once.

Serves 4–6

MOCK DUCK FOO YUNG

2 tablespoons vegetable oil
1 medium onion, shredded
280 g canned vegetarian mock duck,
    thinly sliced
60 g green peas, blanched
60 g corn kernels, cooked
6 eggs, beaten
salt and pepper
1 tablespoon light soy sauce
60 g vermicelli noodles, fried and
    lightly crushed
1 shallot, shredded

Heat oil in a pan. Add onion and stir-fry with mock duck, peas and corn 2 minutes. Stir in eggs, salt, pepper and soy sauce. Draw edges of mixture into the centre until set, without allowing mixture to dry.

Place noodles on a serving platter. Place egg mixture on top leaving a noodle border. Top with shallot shreds.

Serves 8

*Mock Duck Foo Yung (above) and
Crunchy Omelette in a Nest (below)*

STEAMED DIM SUM

24 wonton skins
lettuce leaf, for steaming

FILLING

250 g firm bean curd, finely chopped
125 g soy beans, cooked and mashed
1 shallot, finely cut
1 tablespoon chopped fresh coriander
    leaves
2 tablespoons celery, finely chopped
2 Chinese mushrooms, soaked in
    warm water 20 minutes and chopped
2 teaspoons soy sauce
¼ teaspoon sesame oil
salt and pepper

Combine all filling ingredients. Place 2
teaspoons filling onto each wonton skin.
Gather outer edges of skin around filling.
Press gently so that filling rises to the top
of skin. The base should be flat. Place a
lettuce leaf in steamer. Arrange dim sum
on top, leaving space between each to
prevent sticking. Steam 10 minutes.
Serve with soy vinegar dip.

Makes 24 dim sum

VEGETABLE CHOW MEIN

1 ½ cups vegetable oil (375 mL)
250 g fresh noodles
2 tablespoons vegetable oil
½ teaspoon chopped garlic
1 small onion, shredded
1 medium carrot, sliced and parboiled
160 g bamboo shoots, sliced
150 g mini corn
8 fresh mushrooms, thickly sliced
200 g fresh mustard cabbage, cut
    into 3 cm lengths (see Glossary)
1 tablespoon soy sauce
½ cup vegetable stock (125 mL)
1 tablespoon cornflour blended with
¼ cup vegetable stock (60 mL)

Heat oil in a pan. Add one-third of the
noodles. Fry until crisp, turning over with
tongs during cooking. Drain well and
repeat until noodles are cooked. Set
aside on a warm serving platter.

Heat 2 tablespoons oil. Add garlic,
onion, carrot, bamboo shoots and corn.
Stir-fry 1 minute. Add mushrooms, cabbage, soy sauce and stock. Cook
covered 2 minutes.

Stir in blended cornflour and stock to
thicken. Serve hot over fried noodles.

Serves 4–6

BEAN CURD OMELETTE

2 tablespoons vegetable oil
¼ teaspoon salt
2 shallots, finely chopped
60 g peas, blanched in boiling water 1
    minute
125 g bean curd, cut in 1 cm dice
6 eggs, beaten
1 tablespoon light soy sauce

Heat oil in a wok. Add salt, shallots, peas
and bean curd. Stir-fry 1 minute. Pour in
eggs. Cook over medium heat until mixture begins to set. Draw outer edges to
the centre until eggs form a scrambled
egg consistency, moist and retaining
shape. Sprinkle with soy sauce before
serving.

Serves 4–6

VEGETARIAN ABALONE WITH MUSHROOMS

1 tablespoon vegetable oil
¼ teaspoon salt
8 medium mushrooms, cut into 1 cm
    slices
1 cup bamboo shoots, sliced (150 g)
1 tablespoon dry sherry
2 teaspoons light soy sauce
280 g canned vegetarian abalone, sliced
2 medium shallots, cut into 2 cm lengths
2 teaspoons cornflour blended with
1 tablespoon vegetable stock

Heat oil, add salt, mushrooms and bamboo shoots. Stir-fry 2 minutes. Add
sherry, soy sauce and vegetarian abalone slices. Simmer 3–4 minutes
covered. Fold in shallots. Thicken with
blended cornflour if desired.

Serves 4–6

BARBECUED BEAN CURD

250 g firm bean curd
3 tablespoons Char Sui marinade (see
    recipe)

Pierce bean curd with toothpick. Coat
evenly with char sui sauce and marinate
30 minutes.

The bean curd can be oven-roasted
Chinese style for 20 minutes at 175°C
(340°F) or pan-fried in 3–4 tablespoons
oil, turning onto each side during cooking.

Cool and slice. Use for stir-fry combinations, soups or in fried rice.

Makes 250 g

STIR-FRIED HONEY DUCK

280 g can vegetarian mock duck
2 teaspoons vegetable oil
½ teaspoon chopped garlic
2 shallots, sliced
1 ½ tablespoons light soy sauce
1 ½ tablespoons dry sherry
1 tablespoon honey
1 teaspoon cornflour blended with
2 teaspoons stock

Cut mock duck into even-sized 2–3 cm
pieces.

Heat oil in a pan. Add garlic and shallots and stir-fry 1 minute. Add soy sauce,
sherry and honey, simmer 2 minutes.
Add vegetarian duck pieces and simmer
15 minutes. Thicken with blended cornflour and stock.

Serves 4

BEAN CURD AND POTATO ROLLS

250 g boiled potato, mashed
250 g firm bean curd, mashed and
    drained
2 shallots, finely chopped
salt and pepper
2 large spring roll skins
cold water or egg white
oil, for deep frying

Combine potato, bean curd, shallots, and
salt and pepper in a bowl. Halve mixture
and shape each half into a roll, 10 cm
long.

Arrange spring roll skins in a diamond
shape. Brush edges with cold water or
egg white. Place one roll on each skin.
Fold lowest point of skin over filling and
roll once. Fold left and right points into
centre. Brush edges again. Roll up firmly
to cook.

Fry in oil to cover until golden and
crisp.

To cook using the oven method, place
rolls onto baking tray and bake at 200°C
(400°F) for 20 minutes until golden.

Serves 4–6

VEGETABLE SPRING ROLLS

2 tablespoons vegetable oil
6 medium, Chinese mushrooms,
    soaked in warm water 20 minutes and
    sliced
2 medium onions, sliced
½ teaspoon chopped garlic
1 teaspoon chopped fresh ginger root
300 g Chinese cabbage, shredded
100 g celery, sliced
100 g beans, sliced
100 g carrot, grated
60 g soy bean sprouts
100 g water chestnuts
3 tablespoons light soy sauce
1 teaspoon sesame oil
pinch pepper
1 tablespoon cornflour blended with
    2 tablespoons vegetable stock
12 large spring roll skins
1 egg white or 2 tablespoons water
100 g firm bean curd, sliced
4 tablespoons plum sauce

Heat oil in a wok. Fry mushrooms,
onions, garlic and ginger 1 minute. Add
remaining vegetables and stir-fry 2 minutes. Blend in soy sauce, sesame oil and
pepper.

Stir in blended cornflour and vegetable
stock to thicken pan juices. Place mixture
on a tray to cool. Divide filling into twelve
portions.

Arrange spring roll skins in diamond
shapes with pointed end towards you.
Brush edges with egg white. Place a
portion of filling onto each skin, top with
sliced bean curd. Fold lower point over
filling. Fold left and right points into
centre. Brush with egg white again. Roll
up firmly and stand on sealed edge.

Rolls can be deep fried two or three at
a time in vegetable oil until golden, or
oven-baked at 180°C (350°F) for 15–20
minutes. Serve with warm plum sauce.

Serves 4–6

VEGETARIAN DUCK WITH MUSHROOMS

2 teaspoons vegetable oil
125 g fresh mushrooms, cut 1 cm
    slices
pinch five spice powder
1 teaspoon light soy sauce
280 g canned vegetarian mock duck

Heat oil in a pan. Add mushrooms, five
spice powder and soy sauce. Simmer 1
minute. Add mock duck and continue
cooking 10–15 minutes, covered. Serve
hot over stir-fried Chinese cabbage.

Serves 4

SWEET AND SOUR BEAN CURD

500 g firm bean curd, cut in 2 cm dice
1 tablespoon soy sauce
1 tablespoon dry sherry
2 teaspoons sugar
½ teaspoon salt
1 egg, beaten
2–3 tablespoons cornflour
½ teaspoon five spice powder
    (optional)
1 ½ cups vegetable oil for deep frying
    (375 ml)
1 onion, cut into eighths
½ red capsicum, cut into 2 cm dice
½ green capsicum, cut into 2 cm dice
1 stalk celery, cut into 2 cm dice
200 g unsweetened pineapple pieces

SAUCE

½ cup white vinegar (125 ml)
3 tablespoons sugar
2 teaspoons tomato sauce
½ teaspoon chopped fresh ginger root
1 cup pineapple juice (125 ml)
1 tablespoon cornflour

Combine bean curd with soy sauce,
sherry, sugar and salt. Let stand 15 minutes. Drain bean curd, and mix with
beaten egg.

Roll diced bean curd in a mixture of
cornflour and five spice powder.

Deep-fry bean curd until golden; drain.
Reheat 1 tablespoon oil. Stir-fry vegetables and pineapple 3 minutes.

To make sauce, blend all sauce
ingredients in saucepan. Stir over moderate heat until boiling and thickened. Combine with bean curd and vegetable mixture and heat through.

Serves 6–8

PRESERVED RED GINGER GARNISH

250 g fresh ginger root, shredded
1 tablespoon salt
2 cups vinegar (500 mL)
1 cup sugar (250 g)
1 teaspoon red food colouring

Sprinkle ginger with salt and stand 2
hours. Rinse thoroughly and drain.

Heat vinegar in a wok and stir in sugar
until it dissolves. Add ginger, cover and
simmer gently for about 10 minutes.
Remove from the heat, add food colouring and stir. Let cool completely. Transfer
to a sterilised jar, cover and refrigerate.

Preserved red ginger will keep for at
least 1 year or longer. Use for garnishing.

Makes about 3 cups (750 mL)

Ginger

SHANGHAI MOCK DUCK

280 g canned vegetarian mock duck
2 shallots, sliced
1 teaspoon chopped fresh ginger root
1 clove star anise or pinch five spice
  powder
1 tablespoon soy sauce
2 teaspoons dry sherry
2 teaspoons sugar
½ cup vegetable stock (125 ml)

Place mock duck and remaining ingredients into a saucepan. Bring to the boil, then simmer 15–20 minutes, stirring occasionally.

Mixture can be thickened slightly with blended cornflour if you wish. Remove star anise before serving with steamed rice.

Serves 4

Tossed Rice Noodles with Chop Suey

TOSSED RICE NOODLES WITH CHOP SUEY

3 tablespoons vegetable oil
1 teaspoon chopped fresh ginger root
1 onion, shredded
100 g broccoli florets
½ cup vegetable stock (125 mL)
250 g fresh mushrooms, cut in 1 cm
  slices
200 g bean sprouts, root removed
160 g bamboo shoots, sliced
60 g water chestnuts, sliced
300 g bean curd cakes, diced
2 tablespoons dry sherry
1 teaspoon sesame oil
450 g rice noodles, sliced

GARNISH

1 egg omelette, cut into thin strips
1 shallot, finely chopped
1 tablespoon almond slivers, toasted

Heat oil in a wok. Add ginger, onion and broccoli, and stir-fry 1 minute. Add stock and cook covered 2 minutes. Add mushrooms, bean sprouts, bamboo shoots, water chestnuts, bean curd, sherry and sesame oil. Fold in noodles. Cover and simmer 1–2 minutes to heat through. Serve hot.

Garnish with shredded egg, shallot and almond slivers.

Serves 4–6

MOCK DUCK

First made in China in the Tenth Century AD, mock duck is made from wheat flour, gluten, safflower oil, soy bean extract, sugar, salt and water. Considered a delicacy, it is available canned, and can be used to replace real duck in most recipes.

Delicious Desserts, Chinese-Style

Chinese cuisine is not so well known for its sweets, yet there are some delicious ways to end your own private banquet and satisfy the family sweet tooth. Children love Toffee Apples, more sophisticated palates may prefer Mandarin Sorbet, while dinner party guests will love the spectacularly colourful Eight Precious Pudding.

MANDARIN SORBET

500 g mandarins
250 g caster sugar
450 mL water
2 egg whites

Peel mandarins. Using a teaspoon, scrape the underside of the skin to remove any white pith from the zest. Cut the zest into thin strips. Combine zest, sugar and water in a saucepan. Heat until sugar completely dissolves. Raise heat and boil syrup for 5 minutes. Remove from heat and cool completely.

Squeeze juice from mandarins and strain. Strain syrup and combine with mandarin juice. Freeze mixture until partially frozen, stirring occasionally.

Whisk egg whites until stiff. Beat into soft ice mixture. Freeze until ice is firmer. Whisk again until smooth. Return to freezer until firm. Remove with small ice cream scoop.

Serves 4–6

LYCHEE AND GINGER MOUSSE

400 g canned lychees, drained
(reserve 2 tablespoons juice)
1 tablespoon ginger in syrup, drained
and chopped, (reserve 1
tablespoon syrup)
2 teaspoons gelatine
300 mL thickened cream, whipped
3 egg whites, beaten

Chop most of the lychees with ginger. Place gelatine in a heatproof bowl, add reserved lychee juice and dissolve over hot water.

Lightly fold cream into egg whites. Add lychee mixture, reserved ginger syrup and gelatine, until well combined.

Pour into six individual glasses and refrigerate until set. Top with remaining fruit and rosettes of cream.

Alternatively, the mixture can be set in a wetted ring mould and served whole, garnished with extra fruit and cream.

Serves 4–6

RAMBUTAN COCKTAIL

565 g canned rambutan fruit, drained
400 g honey-dew melon balls
400 g rock melon balls
1 tablespoon orange liqueur
1 egg white
¼ cup caster sugar (50 g) mixed with a
few drops green food colouring
chilled sparkling white wine

Combine fruit and liqueur. Place egg white and sugar on two separate plates. Invert six dessert glasses and dip rim into egg white, then into coloured sugar. Fill glasses with assorted fruit and liqueur. Cover with sparkling wine. Serve chilled.

Note: Rambutan is a bright red fruit, oval in shape, which comes from Malaysia. It is available fresh or canned at supermarkets. If you need to substitute, you can use lychees or mangosteen.

Serves 4–6

Mandarin Sorbet (above) and Lychee and Ginger Mousse (below)

FRESH FRUIT ROLLS

1 firm ripe mango, peeled and cut in 2 cm
  dice
3 slices ripe fresh pineapple, peeled and
  cut in 2 cm dice
1 large apple, peeled and cut in 2 cm
  dice
3 kiwi fruit, peeled and cut in 2 cm dice
3 firm bananas, peeled and cut in 2 cm
  dice
200 g strawberries
3 teaspoons orange liqueur
6–8 large spring roll skins
1 egg white, beaten
vegetable oil, for frying
icing sugar
vanilla ice cream

Combine fruit in a bowl. Sprinkle with
liqueur and stand 15 minutes; drain.

Divide fruit between spring roll skins.
Brush edges with egg white. Roll up as
for ordinary spring rolls.

Fry three rolls at a time in oil to cover.
When golden, remove and drain well.

Dust with icing sugar and serve with
ice cream.

Serves 6–8

FRIED FRUIT BON BONS

100 g dried apricots, finely chopped
100 g dates, finely chopped
50 g crystallised ginger, finely chopped
90 g pecan nuts or cashews, chopped
1 ½ teaspoons chopped orange zest
3 teaspoons orange liqueur or orange
  juice
200 g wonton skins
vegetable oil, for frying
icing sugar

Combine apricots, dates, ginger, pecans,
orange zest and liqueur. Roll a tablespoon of filling in hands until 2.5 ×
0.8 cm in diameter.

Place filling across wonton wrapper.
Moisten edges with water. Roll up to
seal, twisting ends.

Fry Bon Bons in oil to cover until crisp.
Drain well. Dust with icing sugar and
serve with Chinese tea.

Serves 4–6

TOFFEE APPLES

4 ripe apples
1 egg
1 egg white
2 tablespoons plain flour
2 tablespoons cornflour
oil, for deep frying
¼ cup vegetable oil (60 mL)
¼ cup sugar (60 g)
¼ cup honey (90 g)
1 ½ tablespoons white sesame seeds
  (optional)
1 bowl iced water

Peel and core apples and cut each apple
in six to eight wedges. Beat egg and egg
white together and fold in sifted flour and
cornflour to make a batter.

Heat oil for deep-frying. Dip apple
wedges in batter and deep-fry until
golden. Remove and drain on absorbent
kitchen paper.

In a saucepan heat vegetable oil, add
sugar and heat, stirring constantly, until
sugar dissolves. Stir in honey.

Coat apple fritters with syrup and
sprinkle with sesame seeds.

Serve while piping hot. Let each guest
dip apple fritters into iced water. This will
cause the syrup coating to harden so the
fritters will be crisp and crackling on the
outside.

Note: Toffee apples can be prepared to
the stage of dipping in the syrup.

Serves 4

SNOW BALLS

2 cups glutinous rice flour (250 g)
¼ cup cornflour (60 g)
2 tablespoons caster sugar
1 tablespoon lard
¾ cup water (180 mL)
85 g red bean paste
60 g cashew nuts, chopped
2 cups desiccated coconut (190 g)
cherries or strawberries, to garnish
  (190 g)

Combine rice and cornflour with sugar.
Rub in lard, add water and stir with a knife
to form a dough. Knead 2–3 minutes.
Roll dough into a sausage shape and divide into 16 pieces. Shape into balls.

Combine bean paste and cashew nuts.
Divide into 16 portions. Make an inden-
tation or hollow in each dough ball. Fill
each with paste mixture, draw edges
together to enclose filling. Reshape into a
ball. Cook in boiling water 8 minutes, stirring gently to prevent sticking on bottom
of saucepan. Remove balls with a
strainer. Cool slightly, then roll in coconut. Decorate each with half a cherry or
strawberry. Store at room temperature.

VARIATION:
1 cup of coconut can be lightly toasted.
Roll half the balls in each cup coconut.

Serves 4–6

EIGHT PRECIOUS PUDDING

2 cups uncooked long-grain rice (400 g)
250 g assorted dried and glace fruits
    and nuts
1 litre water
220 g sugar
6 tablespoons lard
120 g red bean paste
1 cup water (250 mL)
1 teaspoon almond essence
1 tablespoon cornflour blended with
    3 tablespoons cold water

Wash rice and drain. Prepare fruit and nuts (see Note).

Place rice in a wok, add 4 cups water and bring to the boil. Reduce heat, cover and cook over low heat for about 25 minutes or until dry and fluffy. Cool slightly and add ¼ cup sugar (60 g) and 4 tablespoons lard. Grease a heatproof bowl or dish generously with remaining melted lard. Allow to cool. Arrange fruits and nuts in an attractive pattern over base and sides of bowl pressing lightly into the lard.

Carefully fill bowl with half the rice, pressing gently. Spread with a layer of bean paste, keeping within 3–4 cm of sides. Add remaining rice and press down gently so the pudding will hold its shape when it is unmoulded.

Cover with greased foil and steam 1 hour. Remove bowl from steamer and invert pudding onto a serving plate. Heat 1 cup water (250 mL), remaining sugar and almond essence, until sugar dissolves. Bring to the boil. Add blended cornflour and water to boiling syrup and stir until thickened. Pour sauce over pudding and serve hot or cold.

Note: The original Chinese recipe uses dried and preserved fruits and nuts which are not generally obtainable outside China. They can be relaced, however, by your choice of dried or glace fruits, such as prunes, raisins, sultanas, dates, cherries, apricots and orange peel, and nuts such as almonds, walnuts, lotus seeds and melon seeds. It is best to have at least eight different items to justify the name of the pudding. Nuts should be blanched and halved. The fruits should be pitted and halved or quartered, if large. Fruits, especially glace fruits, can be cut into half moon or other patterns to make an attractive decoration.

Serves 8

Eight Precious Pudding

LEMON GRASS JELLY PARFAIT

540 g canned lemon grass jelly cut in
    2 cm cubes
1 cup dried fresh mango
1 cup strawberries
2 kiwi fruit peeled, cut into 2 cm dice

SOY MILK CUSTARD

2 tablespoons custard powder
600 mL soy milk
3 tablespoons sugar

To make custard, blend custard powder into soy milk. Heat until mixture thickens, stirring occasionally. When boiling, stir in sugar to dissolve.

Combine jelly cubes with fruit. Place a little fruit mixture into each of six parfait glasses. Top with custard and repeat. Finish with a third layer of fruit mixture.

ALMOND FLOAT

2½ cups milk (625 mL)
¼ cup sugar (60 g)
almond essence
1½ tablespoons gelatine
½ cup water (125 mL)
selection of prepared fresh fruit
canned lychees

Scald milk, remove from heat and add sugar. Cool slightly then add almond essence; cool. Sprinkle gelatine over water and leave until water is absorbed. Dissolve gelatine over hot water and cool. Stir into milk mixture.

When ready to serve, cut almond gelatine into diamond shapes. Place fruit in a serving bowl, arrange diamond shapes on top and serve.

Serves 4

Almond Float

MONGOLIAN RICE PUDDING

4 tablespoons brown rice
1 cup water (250 mL)
2 ½ cups milk or soy milk (625 mL)
½ cup sugar (125 g)
½ cup walnuts coarsely chopped (60 g)
¼ cup raisins (40 g)
cinnamon or nutmeg

Put rice and water in a saucepan. Cook until water has been absorbed. Add milk and sugar and cook over low heat until mixture thickens. Add walnuts and raisins to heat through.

Serve hot, sprinkled with cinnamon.

Serves 6

ALMOND AND CASHEW NUT COOKIES

1 cup lard (250 g)
1 cup caster sugar (220 g)
1 egg, beaten
2 tablespoons ground almonds
2 tablespoons ground cashew nuts
½ teaspoon vanilla
½ teaspoon almond essence
2 ½ cups plain flour (310 g)
1 ½ level teaspoons baking powder
pinch salt

Cream lard and sugar together in a bowl. Add egg, almonds, cashews, vanilla and almond essence.

Sift flour, baking powder and salt together. Fold into creamed mixture and knead lightly. Shape dough into walnut-sized balls. Arrange on lightly greased trays. Press each ball to flatten slightly with a fork.

Bake at 200°C (400°F) until pale golden, 15–20 minutes.

Makes about 24

BLACK RICE PUDDING

1 cup black glutinous rice, rinsed in cold water (200 g)
2 ½ cups cold water (625 mL)
565 g canned jackfruit, cut in 1 cm dice, retain juice
420 mL canned coconut cream

Combine rice and water in a large saucepan. Cook until water boils. Lower heat, cover with a lid, and cook 20–30 minutes until rice is tender.

Rinse rice with warm water to separate the grains. Place in a bowl with jackfruit and juice, and coconut cream. Serve chilled in dessert glasses.

Note: This recipe also tastes delicious made with canned or fresh mango instead of jackfruit.

Serves 6

Almond and Cashew Nut Cookies

ASSORTED FRUIT FRITTERS

1 large firm mango, peeled
4 firm bananas, peeled
4 slices fresh pineapple
plain flour, for dusting
¼ teaspoon cinnamon

BATTER

2 cups plain flour (250 g)
1 teaspoon baking powder
¼ teaspoon salt
150 mL milk
150 mL cold water
vegetable oil, for deep-frying
icing sugar
ice cream

Cut fruit into serving pieces. Combine flour and cinnamon and lightly coat fruit, shaking off surplus.

To make batter, sift flour, baking powder and salt into a bowl. Combine milk and water, and beat into flour to form a smooth batter. Strain before using.

Dip fruit into batter and fry in hot oil to cover until golden. Drain well. Arrange on serving platter. Sprinkle with icing sugar. Serve with ice cream.

Serves 6–8

SWEET BEAN PASTE CROQUETTES

165 g canned red bean paste
375 g orange sweet potato
1 tablespoon caster sugar
1 cup glutinous rice flour (125 g)
3 tablespoons poppy seeds
vegetable oil, for frying

Cut bean paste into 16 pieces. Peel sweet potato, slice and steam until tender. Add caster sugar and mash. Mix in glutinous rice flour, adding a little hot water if necessary to make a dough consistency.

Roll dough into a sausage shape, and divide into 16 pieces. Pat each piece of dough into a circle. Place a portion of bean paste in the centre and shape as a croquette (cork shape). Brush each croquette with cold water and roll in poppy seeds.

Heat oil in a pan to the depth of 2 cm. Add six croquette sat a time. Cook over moderate heat 5 minutes turning each roll for even cooking. Avoid overheating the oil, as the croquettes may split. Drain well and serve with Chinese tea.

Serves 4–6

GLOSSARY OF INGREDIENTS AND TERMS

Abalone
(dried, fresh or canned)
Sometimes called mutton fish, it is a large mollusc used in soups, stir-fried dishes and salads. Slice fresh abalone thinly. Abalone only needs to be heated through. It will toughen if overheated. If canned, simmer in sauce to reheat.

Agar Agar
A variety of dried seaweed which resembles vermicelli noodles. It must be soaked before use and can be used to replace gelatine. Available dried in powder and stick shape.

Anise, Star Aniseed
Used for spice flavouring, when braising meats and poultry. Available dried, shaped like an eight pointed star.

Bacon Rashers
Bacon slices.

Bamboo Shoots
Young shoots of the bamboo, cut when just appearing above ground. Available in various sized cans, whole, sliced or braised. Use as a vegetable or in combination dishes.

Bean Curd
Used for hundreds of years in the Chinese cuisine. A bland junket-like product made from white soy beans. Available fresh, in long-life packs, canned and dried and the texture can be firm or soft. Firm textured curd is suitable for braising, deep-frying, in soups, steaming or stir-frying with other ingredients. Soft-textured curd can be used in various fillings or soups, or eaten fresh with a dip sauce. Bean curd can be blanched then refreshed before eating fresh. The dried form requires soaking in warm water before using in soups and as a wrapper. High in protein, easily digested and inexpensive. It is perishable, so store refrigerated in water.

Bean Paste, Red
Red beans are cooked in water with sugar, then pureed. Available canned in various sizes and used as a filling in steamed buns, pastries and puddings.

Bean Sprouts
These are the sprouts of mung peas. They sprout within a few days and can be grown indoors throughout the year. The texture is crisp and the taste delicate. They are cooked briefly in stir-fried dishes and used in salads, soups and vegetable combinations. They are readily available fresh or canned from greengrocers and supermarkets.

Bean Sprouts, Soy
Soy bean sprouts are larger than mung pea sprouts and have a slightly stronger flavour. Blanch in boiling water for 1 minute and refresh in cold water, if using in salads. Can be used to replace mung bean sprouts. Available fresh from Asian grocers.

Beans, Black
These fermented small black soy beans are strongly flavoured. Use in suggested amounts with garlic and ginger in braised dishes, sauces, stir-fried beef, pork, chicken and seafood. Black beans are available both in cans and dried in packets of various sizes. The dried variety are inclined to become salty — store in a jar in a cupboard on opening packet; do not refrigerate.

The canned variety is much milder in flavour, due to the canning process. It is best stored in refrigerator after opening. Soak dried variety in warm water or sherry before using to reduce the salty flavour.

Beans, Yellow
These fermented soy beans are actually light brown. When mashed, they can be stir-fried with garlic and ginger to form a sauce base for chicken, pork and seafood. They are much milder in flavour than black beans. Ready-made sauce is also available canned , refrigerate after opening can.

Beef
Mince: Ground beef.
Blade: Cut of beef next to the shoulder blade, ideal for hot pots and casseroles.
Chuck: Cut of beef taken from between the neck and shoulder blade, ideal for hot pots and casseroles.
Fillet Steak: Piece taken from the underside of the rump and sirloin, which has little fat.
Rump Steak: Cut of beef taken from the hinder part of the animal behind the loin.
Scotch Fillet: Also called ribeye; cut of beef with some of the best muscle meat, taken from near the ribs. It can be roasted in one piece or cut into steaks.

Bicarbonate of Soda
Baking soda, an ingredient in baking powder.

Birds Nests
These famous ingredients are actually the nests of seaside swallows. Nests are made from small fish, seaweed and marine plants, which the swallow collects and pulls apart then mixes with saliva to form a nest, which is very gelatinous and rich in protein and vitamins. As the nest becomes very dry and hard, it must be soaked and boiled for several hours before using. Three grades are available: the most expensive are the whole nests, then broken nests and last, the small nest fragments. Birds nest soup, is served at formal banquets and is considered a delicacy. All grades are sold by weight.

Bitter Melon
(Balsalm Pear)
A green, shiny wrinkled-skinned vegetable, shaped like a small cucumber. The flavour is cool and slightly bitter due to the quinine content. This is a popular summer vegetable sold fresh and canned. The melon can be seeded, filled with a minced filling and steamed. Use in soups or stir-fry with black beans, pork, chicken or seafood.

Black Glutinous Rice
Mainly used in sweet dishes, although its colour, when cooked, adds contrast to vegetables and protein. The cooking time and water absorption is similar to brown rice. When cooked, the rice has a very fragrant aroma and is deep purple to black in colour. In China it is grown in the east along with red and white rice. It is usually sold in 1 kg packets.

Broccoli, Chinese
(gai larn)
This variety has more leaves and less flowers than European broccoli. It is sold in bunches and can be stir-fried as a vegetable or combined with meats and seafood. Avoid overcooking to preserve the deep fresh green colour.

Cabbage
(gai choy)
This has a jade green stalk with darker green leaves and is a compact small cabbage with a slight mustard flavour. Cut into 2–5 cm pieces and use in clear soups.

Cabbage, Celery
(wong ah bark)
This variety has long, white, wide stalks, tightly packed with crinkled green leaves. Used in soup, braised or blanched for cabbage rolls. As this is a large cabbage, it is either sold whole or by half.

Cabbage, Chinese
(bark choy)
This cabbage has long white stems and green leaves. Use in stir-fried dishes. The white and green are cut into 2–5 cm pieces. The white is stir-fried first in a little oil with ginger, then the green leaf is added with salt and sugar and 2

Cabbage, Mustard (choy sum)
tablespoons stock. Cook covered for a few minutes until bright green and crispy tender.
This is a smaller vegetable than bark choy with similar uses. The stalk and green are cut into 5 cm sections, then blanched and served with oyster sauce. It is a popular restaurant dish. Leaves and stalks are separated for cooking, then cut into sections. The stalk is stir-fried first in a little oil and ginger, then the leaf is added with stock, sugar and salt, and quickly steamed,covered. Due to its delicate flavour and bright green colour, it combines well with seafood, poultry and noodle combinations.

Calamari
Squid. Prepare as directed according to a particular recipe.

Capsicum
Sweet peppers, red and green.

Chestnut, Water
This root of a marsh plant resembles a small gladioli bulb. It is often grown as a second crop around the edges of rice fields, as both foods grow in muddy conditions. The chestnut has a crisp, delicate flavour which is similar to apples. The black skin must be peeled off before use and the flesh sliced, diced or minced. Eat raw in salads or include in steamed, deep-fried or stir-fried preparations to give a crisp texture. Chestnuts are available fresh, and whole or sliced in cans.

Chicken
Recipes specify exact weight required e.g. 1.2 kg.

Chicken Seasoning
This seasoning contains a combination of ground herbs and spices which complement poultry. It should be used sparingly during preparation prior to cooking. Usually available in 42 g glass shaker type containers.

Chillies
Use fresh chillies where specified, with great care. Rubber gloves can protect the skin from burning but make sure you never touch your eyes while preparing chilli. As the seeds are the hottest part, these can be removed and discarded if preferred. Used fresh or dried to season dishes cooked in the Szechuan style.

Coconut Desiccated
Shredded coconut.

Cornflour
Cornstarch.

Dates, Red
Red dates are used in soups, braised dishes and desserts. They are soaked in warm liquid to plump them before cooking. Sold in packets.

Dragon Eyes (longans)
Similar to lychee fruit only smaller. Use in sweet and sour sauces, fruit salad, or appetiser cocktails. Available fresh in season and canned in syrup.

Egg, Salted Duck
The fresh duck eggs are soaked in a salt brine for 40 days. They must be cooked before eating. Either boiled or steamed on top of rice, salted eggs can be used for omelette, braised whole, steamed with pork or used for salty egg cake.

Eggplant
Aubergine.

Eggs, Preserved
Called 100 year old eggs. The eggs are coated with a mixture of ashes, lime and salt. They are packed in the ground and allowed to cure for 100 days. The white turns a greyish green and the yolk an orange colour. No cooking is required. Usually served as an hors d'oeuvre.

Essence
Extract.

Fish, Dried, Salted
Various sized fish are dried and salted, either whole or in fillets. Slice thinly, place onto a small plate, add 1–2 tablespoons of vegetable oil and some shredded ginger. Place on top of rice after water is absorbed and steam 20 minutes. Eat with rice.

Fish Maw
This is the dried and deep-fried stomach lining of fish. Must be soaked before use. Has no fish flavour when cooked. Used in soup and pork dishes. The large curved crisp pieces are sold by weight.

Five Spice Powder
Is a combination of star anise, cloves, fennel, cinnamon and anise, used in marinades for roasting pork and poultry. Use sparingly in braises, some batters and to flavour breadcrumbs for coating. Sold in small jars and packets.

Flour
Use plain or all-purpose flour unless otherwise stated.
Self-raising flour: all-purpose flour to which baking powder has been added in the proportions of 1 cup (250 mL) flour : 1 teaspoon (5 grams) baking powder.

Fruit
We specify fresh or canned (tinned), but if no fresh fruit is available, you can substitute canned. The dish may taste slightly different.

Fungus Dried Black and White
The black variety is called chee yee and, when soaked, can be used in place of mushrooms and when cooking soups, stir-fry or simmered and added to salads. The white variety is cooked in a syrup and served as a dessert called "white cloud".

Ginger
Fresh ginger root: available at a greengrocer's or fruiterer's; usually peeled and chopped before using.
Powdered ginger: ground ginger, available in spice jars.

Ginger Root, Fresh
Fresh green ginger root is used extensively in Chinese cooking. It can be pickled, crystallised or preserved in syrup. The dried, ground variety should not be used as a substitute for fresh when cooking Chinese food. Available fresh, or chopped and sliced in jars. Red ginger makes an attractive garnish when shredded.

Ginkgo Nuts
Available in cans for instant use in soups, vegetarian dishes and some puddings.

Glutinous Flour
Made from glutinous rice and ground, this flour is used for pastries and dough products.

Glutinous Rice (nor mu)
Available white and black. The white comes in whole grain form and in packs of flour. Use in desserts, pastries, and various dumplings with sweet and savoury fillings. When cooked, it is very sticky and is also known as sticky rice throughout China and Asia.

Golden Needles
The dried buds of the Tiger Lily. When soaked these are used in vegetarian and poultry dishes.

Golden Syrup
Maple or pancake syrup can be used instead.

Herbs
Our recipes specify whether to use fresh or dried herbs, but if you need to replace fresh herbs with dried, the ratio is one to four: 1 teaspoon of dried to 4 teaspoons (1 tablespoon) of fresh herbs.

Hoisin Sauce
Also called Peking or barbecue sauce. This thick brownish-red sauce is made from soy beans, spices, garlic and chilli. It complements most cooking ingredients — spare ribs, pork, poultry and seafood. It can also be used as a table condiment or a base for dip sauces.

Lamb
Chump Chops: Chops cut from the chump section located between the leg and the loin.
Cutlets: Chops cut from the rib loin; can be grilled, fried or roasted.
Leg Chops: Chops taken from the top of the leg.
Loin Chops: Standard cut of lamb, veal or pork, cut from the upper flank and including the lower ribs.
Rack of Lamb: Cutlets from rib loin section still joined together.
Shanks: Pieces cut from the top part of the legs.

Lemon Grass Jelly
Available in cans. Open at each end and remove jelly in one piece. It can be sliced or diced and served with fruit or added to fruit salad. The dark green colour and soft texture makes an interesting contrast when added to fruits.

Lotus Leaves
The leaves from the water lily plant, available fresh and dried. The fresh leaves are used sparingly, sliced in various dishes to impart flavour and fragrance. Dried leaves are soaked before use and are used for wrapping rice, meat and sweet fillings e.g. sweet bean paste, before steaming.

Lotus Root
The starchy root of the lotus flower, about 5 cm in diameter. When sliced, reveals an attractive pattern of holes running through the length of the root. Used mainly for soups and in braised dishes. When dried, soaking is required before cooking. Available fresh and canned.

Lotus Seed Paste
Available in cans, this paste is used as a filling for sweet buns, moon cakes and puddings. The young seed of the water lily can be eaten raw as a fruit or boiled, mashed and sweetened as with the red beans. The seeds are also used in soups, with braised duck, or can be crystallised.

Lychee (Lichee)
Grows on a tree in tropical areas. It resembles a round red strawberry with a thin shell-like skin. It has white translucent flesh and one black seed. Sweet and delicate in flavour, it is available fresh and canned. Used as a dessert with ice cream, in sweet poultry and pork dishes or sweet and sour sauce.

Mixed Spice
Finely ground spice combination, including allspice, nutmeg and cinnamon; used to flavour cakes and buns.

Mushrooms, Canned
Many varieties of cooked mushrooms are available canned which are suitable to add to stir-fried, braised or vegetable dishes. The variety includes: straw, oyster, abalone mushrooms and champignons.

Mushrooms, Chinese
Choose the thick black variety. Soak in warm stock or water for 20 minutes to soften. Retain stalk for stock pot. Chinese mushrooms retain their shape in cooking. Can be stir-fried, braised, steamed, chopped and added to rice and poultry stuffings. Store in airtight jar.

Noodles, Dried
Dried thin and thick noodles are made from wheat and rice flour, with and without eggs. They are usually cooked in boiling water before frying. Some varieties of rice noodles are soaked in warm water then stir-fried or added to soups. Flavoured noodles are popular and cook quickly e.g. prawn, chicken, beef and curry flavours are available.

Noodles, Fresh
Fresh egg and eggless wheat noodles are available in most Chinese supermarkets. Thin, round and flat as well as spaghetti size are made daily. They can be frozen in recipe size amounts. Fresh rice noodles flavoured with prawns or parsley as well as plain, are available in sheets and strips ready for boiling.

Oil
Use a vegetable or olive oil, unless otherwise specified.

Olive Nuts
These are the kernels of the Chinese olive and their texture is softer than other nuts used in cooking. They are best toasted to a light ivory colour and can be used as a garnish or with mild flavoured dishes. They are approximately 14 mm in length.

Oyster Sauce
Made from fresh oysters, this sauce is used as a flavouring in cooking or served as a table condiment. Available in bottles and cans, it is best to refrigerate after opening.

Parsley, Chinese (coriander)
Fresh coriander has a wonderful aroma when crushed or chopped. It can be used fresh, cooked with other ingredients or used as a garnish. Sold fresh in bunches.

Paw Paw
Papaya or Papaw.

Pickles, Chinese
A combination of ginger, turnip, carrot and cucumber in a pickle syrup. Sold in jars.

Pork
Butterfly chop: Boned, rind removed loin chop or steak, split in half and opened out.
Fillet: Boned, rind removed piece cut from the underside of the rump and sirloin.
Medallions: Rind removed, boned, round pieces taken from the loin.
Spareribs: meat cut from the ribs still containing rib bones.
Steaks: pieces cut from the leg or rump cross the grain of the muscle.
Tenderloin: a very tender strip of meat, part of the loin under the ribs.

Prawn
Shrimp.

Prawn Meat
Green or cooked prawns, with head, tail, shell and intestinal tract removed. Use in stir-fried recipes or where prawns are required.

Pumpkin
Use any type.

Red Beans
Small red beans similar in size to mung beans. When cooked, mashed and sweetened the red bean paste is used in sweet buns, desserts, and puddings. The beans are also available in powder form.

Red Ginger
Fresh young ginger, peeled, sliced and cooked in a red, sugar syrup. Available in jars or cans. Use as a garnish for seafood, rice dishes or desserts.

Rice
Rice is the staple food of the Chinese in southern China. White short-grain is preferred, although brown rice is used in rural areas. Both white and brown rice are available with long and short grains.

Rock Melon
Also known as ogen melon and cantaloupe.

Sausage, Chinese Pork, Liver
Chinese sausages are sold in pairs or pre-packaged packs. The pork variety is a light pink waxed colour; the liver variety is dark. They are both steamed by direct method or on top of rice, before eating or adding to other ingredients. Both varieties are savoury.

Sausage Skins (casings)
These can be purchased at most butcher shops. As they are stored in salt they should be bought in advance, to allow time for soaking in warm water before use. Leftover skin can be frozen.

Seafood Sticks
Sold fresh or frozen. Can be used individually or to extend more expensive seafood dishes. They have a fine white texture and are crab shell red on top surface. 10 x 1.5 cm in shape.

Sesame Oil
Made from sesame seeds, this oil tastes very strong, so use sparingly. Adds flavour to dip sauces, salads, soups, and is rarely used as a cooking oil.

Sesame Paste
Ground toasted sesame seeds, with a peanut butter texture. Used in sauces and available in cans and jars.

Shallots
Very small white onions also known as scallions and spring onions.
Spring onions: larger, white-bulbed sweet onions.

Sharks Fin
Used in thick rich soups, omelettes and in poultry stuffings. It is high in calcium and protein and comes in cans and dried.

Snow Peas
The pods are cooked before the peas mature and add crispness and colour to stir-fried foods. Sold fresh or frozen. Remove tips and string before cooking.

Soy Milk
Available fresh, dried and in long-life packs. The fresh milk is also available flavoured. Refreshing as a drink, it can also be used in cakes, custards and sauces.

Soy Sauce
Essential in Chinese cooking to flavour pork, beef, poultry and fish. Available in dark form for cooking and light form for a table condiment. Salt-reduced soy sauce is also available for special diets.

Spring Roll Skins Available fresh or frozen in large and small sizes. Fresh skins can be re-wrapped and frozen in smaller quantities.

Star Anise *See* Anise, Star Aniseed

Stock Cube Bouillon cube; can be replaced with one teaspoon powdered stock or bouillon.

Sugar Use any sugar you prefer unless otherwise specified. The most common types are the following:
Caster: fine white granulated sugar.
Raw: brown granulated sugar.
Brown: soft, moist sugar.
Icing: confectioner's or powdered sugar.
Sugar slices.

Sugar Slices Rock sugar is sold by weight in packets. This amber coloured sugar, which is available in block form is used in cooking to sweeten. It takes longer to dissolve than crystal sugar.

Veal Chops: taken from the loin and the ribs.
Cutlets: taken from the loin and the ribs.
Escalopes: thin slices, often coated in breadcrumbs and fried.

Vegetarian Mock Duck · Made from wheat flour, gluten, safflower oil, soy bean extract, sugar, salt and water. Sold in 285 g cans. This product was first made in China in the 10th century. A delicacy, it was given the same taste and texture as roast duck, supposedly to keep vegetarians from swaying from their faith. It is a light food which can replace duck in most recipes.

Wonton Skins A thin fresh pastry made from eggs and flour. Sold by weight fresh or frozen. Skins are 8 cm square. Fillings can be made from fresh raw ingredients pork, beef, seafood, poultry or vegetables. They can be deep-fried, steamed, boiled or baked. They can be re-wrapped and frozen.

Wheat Starch A product of China's northern wheat growing areas. Wheat starch is little used in food preparation but is extensively used as a thickening agent. Flour has less thickening power and makes a more opaque gel than cornflour. Its characteristic flavour is preferred by many to that of other thickening agents. It is sold in smaller packets in Chinese food stores.

Yoghurt Use natural or unflavoured yoghurt.

Zucchini Courgette.

EQUIPMENT AND TERMS

CAN, CANNED: tin, tinned.
CRUSHED: minced, pressed.
FRYING PAN: skillet.
GRILL: broil.
GREASEPROOF PAPER: waxproof paper.
LAMINGTON TIN: oven tray 4 cm (1½ inches) deep. Grease and use as a biscuit or cake tin.
PAPER TOWEL: absorbent kitchen paper towel.
PLASTIC WRAP: cling film.
PUNNET: small box or basket containing about 250 g (8 oz) of fruit.
SEEDED: stoned or pitted — stone removed and discarded.
SPRING-FORM CAKE TIN: spring pan or loose-bottomed cake tin.

MEASURES

DRY INGREDIENTS

Metric	Imperial
15 g	½ oz
30 g	1 oz
60 g	2 oz
90 g	3 oz
125 g	4 oz (¼ lb)
155 g	5 oz
185 g	6 oz
220 g	7 oz
250 g	8 oz (½ lb)
280 g	9 oz
315 g	10 oz
345 g	11 oz
375 g	12 oz (¾ lb)
410 g	13 oz
440 g	14 oz
470 g	15 oz
500 g (0.5 kg)	16 oz (1 lb)
750 g (0.75 kg)	24 oz (1½ lb)
1000 g (1 kg)	32 oz (2 lb)

LIQUIDS

Metric	Imperial
30 mL	1 fl oz
60 mL (¼ cup)	2 fl oz (¼ cup)
100 mL	3 fl oz
125 mL (½ cup)	4 fl oz (½ cup)
150 mL	5 fl oz (¼ pt)
185 mL (¾ cup)	6 fl oz (¾ cup)
250 mL (1 cup)	8 fl oz (1 cup)
300 mL (1¼ cups)	10 fl oz (½ pt)
360 mL (1½ cups)	12 fl oz (1½ cups)
420 mL (1¾ cups)	14 fl oz (1¾ cups)
500 mL (2 cups)	16 fl oz (2 cups)
625 mL (2½ cups)	20 fl oz (1 pt)

Oven Temperatures

	Celsius	Fahrenheit	Gas
Very slow	120	250	½
Slow	140–150	275–300	1–2
Moderately slow	160	325	3
Moderate	180	350	4
Moderately hot	190	375	5
Hot	200	400	6
	220	425	7
	230	450	8
Very hot	250–260	475–500	9

LENGTHS

Metric	Imperial
5 mm	¼ in
1 cm	½ in
2 cm	¾ in
2.5 cm	1 in
5 cm	2 in
6 cm	2½ in
8 cm	3 in
10 cm	4 in
12 cm	5 in
15 cm	6 in
18 cm	7 in
20 cm	8 in
23 cm	9 in
25 cm	10 in
28 cm	11 in
30 cm	12 in
46 cm	18 in
50 cm	20 in
61 cm	24 in
77 cm	30 in

Standard Metric Measures

1 cup	= 250 mL
1 tablespoon	= 20 mL
1 teaspoon	= 5 mL

All spoon measurements are level.